GOD'S DONKEY

God's Donkey

Peter Newman

KINGSWAY PUBLICATIONS
EASTBOURNE

First published 1985

ISBN 0 86065 329 3

G. K. Chesterton's poem *The Donkey* is reproduced by kind permission of the publishers, J. M. Dent & Son Ltd.

Front cover photo: Photo Source Ltd

Printed in Great Britain for
KINGSWAY PUBLICATIONS LTD
Lottbridge Drove, Eastbourne, E. Sussex BN23 6NT by
Cox & Wyman Ltd, Reading.
Typeset by Nuprint Services Ltd, Harpenden, Herts.

TO

BARBARA

my wife and fellow traveller
along the ways of God

Contents

THE DONKEY

When fishes flew and forests walk'd
And figs grew upon thorn,
Some moment when the moon was blood
Then surely I was born;

With monstrous head and sickening cry
And ears like errant wings,
The devil's walking parody
On all four-footed things.

The tatter'd outlaw of the earth,
Of ancient crooked will;
Starve, scourge, deride me: I am dumb,
I keep my secret still.

Fools! For I also had my hour,
One far fierce hour and sweet:
There was a shout about my ears,
And palms before my feet.

G. K. Chesterton

Acknowledgements

I would like to take the advantage of this book to acknowledge those that have over the years encouraged me and prayed me through to do the work of an evangelist:

Mr Jack Calverley, Bristol
Mr David Foot Nash, Plymouth (deceased)
Mr Joe Halls, Carkeet, Cornwall
Pastor Fred Sharman, Plympton, Devon
Pastor Jack Keyes, Saltash, Cornwall
Pastor Len Hooper, Downinny, Cornwall
Arthur Burt, North Wales
Mick and Roslie Smith, Swindon, Wilts
Mr and Mrs Mascall, London (deceased)
Mrs Mascall, London
Pam and Harry Greenwood, Chard, Somerset
Tom Snyder, Long Island, New York

My special thanks to Myrtle Shepherd (now deceased) for her love and encouragement as she helped in the preparation of the manuscript. Without her I doubt whether I would even have got started.

Also to Dorothy, whom I now forgive for the persistent questions and grilling she gave me in her marathon effort to put this book together.

Introduction

Today, as I look back at my life, I marvel at the hand of God, lifting me from the slopes of destruction to the heavenly steps of God. The miracles he has worked in me and for me make me feel very humble. I want to bear testimony to over fifty years of God's faithfulness and answered prayer.

These glimpses through the years are a true picture of my background and my life as an evangelist. There are good times and bad times, funny times and sad times. They are set down to encourage those who are already in the call of God and to inspire those who are seeking God. They are to state that 'God is God' and that when he declares in the Bible that he will never leave you nor forsake you, he means it. I want to show that from my experience.

You will see things that should never happen to an evangelist and things that an evangelist should never do. Yet there is the unrelenting call to be an evangelist, with all that such a calling entails.

It is a great and dangerous calling, for the evangelist is marching into enemy territory. He needs to be surrounded by the prayers and love of the church. It is when I have not had this prayer support that things have sometimes gone wrong for me.

When in trouble the evangelist can so easily hit the headlines because he has had to make himself known. The publicity which has brought the crowds to the meeting will just as readily be used against him by the media if something goes wrong.

The preaching of the gospel may rouse anger and emotion in people and in demons. The evangelist may be labelled exhibitionist or big-headed ridiculed as a figure of fun.

He has the task of bringing the people to himself in order that he may then bring them to Jesus. When Peter and John went up to the Temple Gate they said to the man begging there, 'Look on us,' and having gained his attention they exhibited the power of Jesus.

The dictionary describes an evangelist as, 'One who sets out to preach the gospel, to evangelize, to make known the Good News. To preach the gospel from place to place.' It also says that, 'An evangelist is an assistant to an apostle, authorized to preach but without a fixed charge.'

And that raises two questions—who authorized me to preach and gave me my credentials, and who supports me and my family? I trust you will find the answers in the pages that follow.

Peter Newman

I

God's Donkey

I'm a donkey. God's donkey. Most of the time I want to be a race-horse, going, doing and daring for God. I want to preach to thousands, have a world-wide known ministry, evangelize in tents which have ten poles instead of two. I want everyone to know that I'm Peter Newman, God's servant, God's man for the day.

The donkey isn't a particularly attractive animal. He doesn't tell his rider where he should be going. He's only the vehicle. The donkey has no say in his own destiny—he is merely obedient to his rider. In countries like Israel, donkeys are so commonplace that people hardly notice them. It's the person sitting on his back they look at.

When Jesus first told me he wanted to ride on my back like he rode on the back of the ass's colt going into Jerusalem, I was offended.

'People won't see you, Peter,' the Lord said to me. 'They will see me instead.'

'That's all very well, Lord,' I argued. 'But what about me?' Now I knew in theory that I was only a vessel designed to carry a very precious treasure and I knew, like John the Baptist, that I had to decrease so that Jesus within me could increase. My mind knew it all and accepted it all, but my pride thought it was too much to ask.

I've found it far from easy to become the donkey God told me to be. I've kicked against the pricks. I've sulked, fought, objected, wrestled, and then, when I've eventually come to my senses, I've given in.

I used to get discouraged when reading Christian testimony books. They all seemed to be written by such perfect people who, once they were saved, never did anything wrong, never failed God, never stumbled or fell. I've done all of these things, and one truth I've discovered is that God is bigger than our mistakes. I should have known that from reading the Bible. Didn't Moses, the great deliverer, once kill an Egyptian and flee into the back of beyond? And wasn't it there that God dealt with his wilfulness and brought him out as pure gold?

So my story, then, isn't one of a shining, successful Christian who never has doubts, fears or misgivings. But it is one about God's very gracious dealings with an ordinary human being. I like to think that it's a story of hope and assurance—that he who has started a good work in a man will see it through until the day of Jesus Christ.

2

God Makes His Own Arrangements

I picked up the phone to check with the airport. I had barely lifted it to my ear when that inner impression I now knew to be the voice of God spoke to me again: 'I've told you the date to go. You are to leave the house tonight to catch the plane early tomorrow.'

Didn't God know there was a twenty-four hour strike at Heathrow Airport and no planes were either taking off or landing?

My wife Barbara came into the room. 'There's no point in even trying,' she said as I put the phone down again. 'You're only going to have a wasted journey to the airport and a wasted day tomorrow.'

My youngest daughter Sharon also chimed in with the latest news bulletin. 'Grounded for the next 24 hours,' she declared, with a glint in her eye. Perhaps God or Dad had made a mistake this time.

'But I've got to go. God has told me to and that means my flight will be all right.' Barbara was silent for a moment. Then she nodded and started fussing over my cases, making sure everything was there. I got my coat, picked up my luggage, kissed her goodbye and headed off for the train which would take me into London.

I hadn't booked a seat on the plane—whenever God tells me to fly here or there, I just turn up at the airport and get a stand-by ticket. But I didn't expect the queue at the airline office to be as long as it was that morning.

It was chaotic. There were between 250 and 300 tired and irate people waiting. The man in front of me had a transistor radio and was relaying the latest news about the airport strike to one and all.

'Where were you hoping to go?' he asked glumly.

'Chicago,' I replied confidently.

'You must have a ticket.'

'No, stand-by,' I replied.

He started to laugh and said I didn't stand a chance of getting anywhere near Chicago. Others stared at me and winked at one another; at least they had tickets to their destination. I just held my tongue and waited. My turn eventually came. I asked for stand-by to Chicago. The clerk looked oddly at me, hesitated and demanded passport and money. I had my ticket.

The whole section was packed with people. To get to the phone to ring Barbara I had to climb over bodies, suitcases and flight bags. Everyone was fed up with waiting for flights which, according to the latest reports, would never take off.

I dialled Plymouth. 'Hello, Barbara,' I said. 'I'm at the airport. I've got my ticket and I'll be flying within the next couple of hours.'

'Oh,' she said. 'Is the strike over then?'

'No,' I replied, 'but I'll ring you from America. Bye, dear.'

I headed for the departure lounge, which was almost empty. The information boards said that all transatlantic flights were cancelled until further notice. I sat down and waited for some information about my flight to flicker on the electronic board. I can't say I was bursting with faith. All I knew was that God had told me to catch a plane to America and that God makes his own arrangements in spite of man.

I glanced up and, sure enough, details of my flight were coming up on the board. It was leaving, as scheduled. I said a quick 'Thank-you Lord', grabbed my belongings and headed off to the assigned gate. But I wasn't home and dry yet.

'There's very little chance of your getting on with only a stand-by ticket,' the official told me. 'Go over there and wait while everyone else gets on board.'

I joined the two other stand-by ticket holders and we sat and waited. And waited.

What seemed like an age later the official called us over and told us we could board. I expected the jet to be full, but it was almost empty. I smiled to myself. 'Thank-you, Lord,' I repeated as I lay across three empty seats and went to sleep.

A few hours later the pilot's voice came over the intercom. He apologized because we would be one minute late arriving in Chicago. Then he told us that ours was the only transatlantic flight to have left Heathrow on time that day.

I lay back. 'How good God is,' I thought. And I

started thinking about God's wonderful faithfulness to me over the years. Even from the earliest years.

3

'A Thief I'll Be'

My grandad used to be a drunkard. People would make up songs about old Wally Newman who could be seen staggering along the streets of London, night after night after night.

He wasn't a down and out—he had a good business brain even though it was in a state of pickled animated suspension most of the time! No, Grandad owned coffee stalls. He paid men to dish up the brew while he quietly got sozzled on the profits.

His life was dramatically changed the night he walked past a mission hall somewhere in the East End. There was something very different about the singing which drifted through the half-open windows. Now old Wally Newman loved a good sing so in he went, in his usual drunken state, to see what was going on.

He had barely pushed open the doors when he had a vision of Jesus. He broke down, cried and was instantly converted. He stayed for the rest of the service and then went post haste to the Embankment to tell his mates what had happened to him. And he didn't just tell them the once. Day after day he'd go to his old haunts and tell his former drinking pals of the Christ who had cleaned up his life and given him a brand new start. Many of them used to sit and weep with him as he told them of the day he met Jesus. Grandmother, however, wasn't quite so touched by her Wally's experience. She couldn't deny the change in him but she liked a bit of fun herself and she didn't go in for 'all that religious stuff'.

My two sisters and I went to live with my grandparents when we were very small, our own mother having abandoned us when I was only eighteen months old. By this time the converted Wally Newman had a small cottage, called Kosicot in the countryside. I never knew my mother, but my father worked in a nearby town and would come and visit us quite often.

Every night Grandad would say prayers with us, and I will always remember him lining us all up in the garden to teach us the choruses he loved so much. He called Sunday 'the Sabbath' and we all had to be on our best behaviour from getting up to going to bed. The Sabbath was always the longest day of the week.

He would often go out preaching at local chapels and churches. The minute he was out of sight at the lane end, Grandmother would wind up the old gramophone and dance on the lawn, beckoning all of us to join in her forbidden revelries. 'Now don't you go telling Grandad what we're up to,' she would say with a twinkle in her eye. 'This is our little secret.' We'd all nod solemnly and then carry on enjoying ourselves. Grandad never found out about our little games because everything would be back to its usual sober self by the time he walked up the garden path, Bible in hand.

Those were happy days, but storm clouds were gathering on the horizon. Everyone seemed quite pleased when Dad brought this woman to Kosicot to meet Daphne, Clare and me. She seemed quite pleasant and not too many weeks had passed before Dad decided he wanted to marry her. That decision meant a great change in our lives—we kids were going to live with the newly-weds in a big house in town. The prospect of life in town appealed to my eight-year-old mind. We were going to be a real family again—surely life was going to be even better than it had been at Kosicot.

I was in for a rude awakening. My step-mother would have much preferred to build her new life without Dad's three children hanging round her feet. Children to her meant dirt, expense and inconvenience, and she was quick to show her dislike for us. I don't know if my father ever realized how unhappy and insecure we felt. He loved her and I often wondered if he just conveniently turned a blind eye to our unhappiness. With our grandparents we had known kindly discipline and love, but now it was harsh discipline and no love. We lived for our grandmother's visits. But then, for some unknown reason, Grandmother was not allowed to come to the house. Once a week though, we used to meet her secretly when she was in town shopping.

I remember the house was like a palace, but never

like a home. The only time we were allowed in it was for food and bed. We never knew what it was like to sit by the fire or to play indoors. Meal times were frightening; to drop a crumb invoked harsh punishment. Our house gleamed and shone with wax polish. A finger mark was a crime. Other people noticed our unhappiness and would invite us into their houses, but we always had to return home. I sometimes had to be escorted back because I was so afraid. Occasionally neighbours talked of reporting our treatment to the authorities, but nobody got round to doing anything.

As we weren't allowed to spend much time in the house itself, I made the garden shed my second home—or rather, my real and only home. I remember spending hour after hour shut away in my own little world reading anything I could lay my hands on. The real world didn't seem to offer very much so I compensated by immersing myself in books—hundreds of them. My shed was packed with biographies, autobiographies, classics, and 'Penny Dreadfuls', as the cheap novel used to be called.

I stayed out of my step-mother's way as much as I could but she was always accusing me of some misdeed or other. I was regularly punished for crimes I'd never committed. I used to spend hours daydreaming about the day I would escape from that house and all its misery, but I knew I would have to wait until I was a bit older to make the break. Eight was, after all, a little young.

The same ambition burned within my sisters. When I was ten Clare ran away and never returned.

She was given a home with a farming family and lived happily ever after. Lucky thing, I thought. Daphne was next to escape. She went into service at fourteen to get away from the house, leaving me lonelier than I'd ever been in all my life. By this time I had two step-sisters and their lot seemed much better than mine. I'd long since stopped praying. I reasoned out that if God allowed me to be so unhappy and miserable, he couldn't be the nice, kind person Grandad had said he was. So I couldn't see much point in even trying to talk with him.

The highlight of my week was Saturday when a local farmer used to pay me to do odd jobs round his farm. I loved the countryside and I loved earning a bit of cash, even though all of it had to be ceremoniously handed over to my step-mother each week. In return she would give me a few pence back and I'd spend it on the luxuries of life, like sweets and books. One Saturday I'd worked especially hard and the farmer gave me a bit of extra money which I kept for myself. I remember hiding it away in my shed, taking it out every now and again to look at it. But my secret didn't stay hidden away for long. My step-mother unearthed my little treasure, assumed that I'd stolen it, and told everyone that I was a thief.

'Right,' I said to myself, fighting back the tears, 'if she says I'm a thief, then a thief I'll be.' And I started stealing things from school. I was never discovered and I soon became a dab-hand at relieving both teacher and pupils of whatever I fancied.

My dishonest actions were temporarily halted when I had an accident in the schoolyard and broke my leg. I remember the headmaster sending for my step-mother and then driving us both home. He assumed that she would make sure my leg received medical attention. It got some attention all right, but not the sort it needed. She was so angry at this disruption of her daily routine that she beat me across the leg. To this day I can remember the pain of that thrashing.

Whenever I complained that my leg hurt and that I couldn't walk on it, she would hit me again. I don't know what my father was doing or thinking during this time, but he certainly didn't do anything to help me. I remember trying to walk to school. My leg was swollen up like a balloon and I used to drag it painfully behind me.

One day a lady came out of her house to ask me what was wrong. I just said that I'd sprained my ankle. She was quite horrified. She took me into her home and called for the doctor who came and treated me. While we were waiting for him to arrive, she told me that she lived with her sister and that both of them were nurses. 'We hold a Bible class in our home every week. If you'd care to come along you'd be very welcome,' she told me. How could I refuse her offer when she'd shown me such kindness?

My step-mother didn't mind my going to the class—after all, if I was in someone else's home then hers couldn't be messed up. So I became a regular attender and I was soon enthralled by the Bible stories I heard there. Joshua particularly appealed to me—and the fact that twelve tribes of Israel left twelve stones to mark their crossing over the river

Jordan impressed me no end.

'Miss,' I called out enthusiastically, 'if those stones are still there I'm going to see them one day.' And see them I did—thirty years later I stood at the place where those stones were laid.

I later met my Bible teacher and we had a good laugh when I told her that my childlike words of prophecy had been fulfilled!

Things at home weren't getting any better and I was still deeply unhappy. Even the joys of the Bible class couldn't compensate for the following six days. So I decided to run away, never, ever to return.

And run away I did. I slept a couple of nights in barns and then made my way to another town not many miles from where I lived. Once there I headed for the railway station, determined to hop on the first train which pulled in. A curious porter, however, had other ideas. I suppose I must have looked a bit suspicious—after all, pint-sized eleven-year-olds don't usually hang around station platforms in the middle of the night.

He called in the police. The officer who questioned me seemed to tower over me from a very great height. I was cold, tired, hungry and the copper seemed to feel a bit sorry for me. I remember him taking me to the police station and giving me a cup of piping hot cocoa. They didn't quite know what to do with me but the policeman who had 'arrested' me said that as he was going off-duty he would take me to his home then contact my parents the following day.

So off we went. His home was lovely—I remember thinking how cosy it was, and lived-in. His wife didn't bat an eye-lid when she saw me—it seemed the most natural thing in the world that her husband should bring a young visitor back in the middle of the night. She made me some supper and as they talked to me, I discovered they were both Christians. They asked me questions about myself and my home life and they read something out of the Bible and prayed with me. Then they took me up to bed and as I drifted off to sleep, I longed to stay in that warm house for ever and ever.

Morning dawned—and with it the awful knowledge that I'd be going back to that big old house to face my step-mother. Someone must have been praying, though, because she didn't give me the hiding I was expecting.

4

A Menace to Society

in days I was off again—this time steering clear vns and policemen. I took to the open road and t in barns. I can't remember being afraid of the ountryside at night—I was just glad to be away from my step-mother and that big old house.

The barns were a good place to stay. Early each morning the farmworkers would arrive and hang up their food bags before going out into the fields. I would peer over the tops of the hay bales and when the last one had gone outside to do his daily work, I would swing down from the loft and tuck into my breakfast. The wives of those men will never know how much I appreciated their cheese sandwiches, cakes and biscuits. To a hungry eleven-year-old, they were like manna from heaven. I wonder who got the blame when the workers discovered their lunches were missing?

If it rained really hard and there wasn't a nearby shed or barn to shelter in, I would make a den in a ditch and cover it over with branches, leaves and grass. Imagine my horror one day when a stranger in an army uniform unearthed my crouched body from my hideaway. Visions of police stations and endless questions flashed through my mind but the army sergeant didn't hand me over to the authorities. Instead he smuggled me into a nearby German prisoner-of-war camp. So I became a German prisoner of war.

For several days he brought me food and tea, but an officer soon discovered my existence and almost before I knew it, I was back with my grandparents at Kosicot. By then I was rebellious and insolent and even Grandad despaired of me. During the day I would sneak on to a nearby American airbase and steal whatever I could get my hands on. Life at Kosicot was boring after my travels on the open road and I couldn't stomach all that religious stuff from my grandad. Those happy Bible class days were a long way off—I was different now and didn't need all that soppy stuff. After a few weeks I grabbed a handful of biscuits and headed off into the countryside again.

I had a wonderful sense of freedom as I sauntered up and down the country lanes. I was my own boss, answerable to no one. Sometimes, for fun, I would steal some penny bangers and go off into the woods at night to set them off. Soon gamekeepers and police would be out hunting for the 'poacher'. I used to run for miles with them all in hot pursuit. When I had had enough fun from my game I used to duck out of the woods, leaving my pursuers chasing shadows. Later on I would turn up at the gamekeeper's cottage, waking him up in the middle of the night by bouncing stones off his corrugated roof. The dogs would bark, and in no time at all the lights would come on, but I was gone.

I could eat when I wanted to, providing some farmworker had left his lunch within reach. Pheasant, chicken and rabbit were often on my menu. I slept where and when I chose. It felt good to be free. I became an artist at relieving people of their goods. I enjoyed the thrill of not only eating and stealing but of being hunted as well.

I decided one night to make a ditch my bedroom so I borrowed a haybale from a local farmer and covered it with some leafy branches. I'd just finished my home when the heavens opened and it started to bucket down. I was happily whiling away the time when suddenly I heard voices. I looked up and saw two pairs of eyes staring at me—I was terrified but determined not to show it.

'What are you doing here, m'lad?' said one of the men who were peering so intently at me. I gave him a mouthful of colourful abuse and told him to mind his own business. My tongue always thought it lived inside a fourteen stone hulk of a body.

'We aren't coming to do you any harm,' said the other man. 'We've been keeping an eye on you over the past few days and we thought we could help you. We weren't thinking of turning you over to the police.'

I was curious, to say the least.

'So who are you, then?' I asked. 'Gypsies, that's what we are,' said one of them with a laugh. 'Come with us and see our caravan.'

'Have you got a horse, as well?' I asked, fascinated at the thought of a real gypsy caravan.

'Yeah, we got a horse,' said the other man. 'Come on with us and we'll show you.'

I needed no further persuasion. We walked through the dark countryside until we came to a clearing. As I was looking round one of the men suggested that I stay with them for a while. They slung some canvas under one of the caravans and made me a hammock.

I soon adapted to their gypsy lifestyle and they taught me many things. I stayed with them for a few months and then joined up with some others.

I still continued to steal, and when I was fifteen the gypsies held a meeting to decide what should be done with me. They knew that my bravado often exceeded my common sense and it was just a matter of time before the police caught me red-handed. And if they caught me, they would doubtless start uncovering a few of the gypsies' illegal activities. I was too big a risk and the gypsies told me I had to leave. I was a bit angry about their decision but I decided it was their loss, not mine, and off I went.

At sixteen I was again in trouble. This time I had to appear at the local magistrates' court. To my amazement a minister appealed to the court on my behalf. He must have made an impression because I was only given probation.

It turned out that the minister felt it was his mission to lead me to higher ground. He took me for a meal and told me that I was being prayed for. I thought that was a cheek: I didn't want older people taking over my life. After the meal he took me home with him. When his wife saw me there was an unholy row. She declared that if I stayed, then she'd go. While they were arguing I decided to settle the affair and leave—with the minister's overcoat under my arm.

School for me was one long punishment. I was dressed in the most weird home-made clothes and was considered a joke by most of the other children. I loved to learn and was once punished for asking too many questions. When I was given the chance of sitting the grammar school entrance exam, I took home extra homework, but it was made quite plain to me that lack of money would prevent me from ever going to a grammar school. So I rebelled again. I stopped doing homework and decided to quit school altogether. I was beaten, taken to the local police station and locked up for the day. This was to frighten me but it only served to turn me into a hero in the eyes of the other children. I preferred to be in prison than submit to the school system.

For quite some time I'd been remembering Grandad's tales about life in London, and when I was sixteen I headed for the city to see if I could make a decent living for myself. Grandad had often talked about all the rich nobs in the West End, so surely any self-respecting thief should be able to nick a few pounds a day to keep body and soul together.

Life in the City scared me a bit at first. Everything seemed to move so fast and while I was familiar with hedgerows and barns, all those tall, rather stately buildings seemed to crowd in on me. But I didn't intend to be licked—London wasn't going to intimidate Peter Newman.

Soho fascinated me. I used to spend hours watching the people on its bustling streets. I soon discovered who would buy what from me and so I started a new chapter in my life of crime. Before long I had a lucrative little business under way, with the profits mostly going on drink. The police were more formidable than the ones in the quiet, country towns and villages and so I was wise enough to wait until dark before I broke into offices and flats. Most of the day was spent sleeping wherever I could find a place to lay my head.

London opened my eyes to crime in a new way. One thing I quickly learned was that one couldn't be a one man band. Crime was controlled from one area to another and there wasn't any chance of operating in an area without the sanction of the 'Boss'. It was difficult to work out who the 'Boss' was and, just to make things more difficult, some areas had more than one. Rivalry between gangs for possession of a 'patch' was fierce and often dangerous. Once you were involved with a gang it was for good. There was no way out.

I was vetted by many gangs, but somehow managed to stay out of full commitment. I became a minder, protecting prostitutes working in certain areas and took my money from their earnings. This was a highly risky occupation—you were in danger from the law on one hand and from rival gangs on the other. In my day the gangs were highly organized. Gang members were mostly foreigners from Mediterranean countries and to tread on their toes meant death! My life became a game of hide and seek. I was a good hustler. People began to take notice of me. But it was taking its toll on my life. Drink and drugs, uppers and downers made me nervous and jumpy. One day I did a very sensible thing—without telling anybody I disappeared into the country. I knew too much to get permission, so I just left—for the quiet life.

I left on the spur of the moment without any thought of my destination. I boarded a train at King's Cross without a ticket and left the rest to British Rail. The journey turned out to be a short one at a place called Sandy.

Somehow I had to leave the station without being caught. A glance around soon had me scrambling up an embankment just outside the station. I disappeared into the night, catching the sound of two men shouting, whom I could just see to be a porter and a policeman.

I was off again, this time to the Home Counties, East Anglia, the Midlands, and finally to the North-West of England.

Eventually I found myself back in court. The judge found me guilty of stealing 6d (2½p) and I was sent to prison to await sentence. One night I was taken before the Governor of the prison. This was very unusual and I noticed that all the customary formalities were done away with. I was invited to sit down and offered a cigarette, which I quickly took. I was very suspicious but it turned out that the Governor was compiling a report for the courts and only wanted to help me. However, I wasn't going to have his help and I told him so.

The day before I was sentenced I was handed a sheet of paper. What I read was my life story, from four years to twenty-two. It wasn't very nice reading. I felt confused and angry that so much could be known about me. None of it was good, but what really stunned me was the last paragraph which read something like this:

> This man has refused any help of rehabilitation and there seems no chance that he will ever fit into society. His anti-social behaviour makes him a menace to society. It is recommended that he be locked away for the protection of others and their property.

The courtroom listened patiently as my solicitor did his best to jerk a few tears from one and all. Then he sat down and the judge started to speak: 'If you are hoping to save this man from going to prison, you may like to know that I have no intention of sending him there. Peter Newman, you will be fined £25. But let me give you this warning. If you appear before any court again you will be imprisoned for at least four years.'

I could hardly take in what he was saying. My heart was pounding so loudly that I was sure everyone in the court could hear it.

'Next case,' the judge called out. 'You are free to go, Mr Newman.'

Free to go—the words spun around in my mind. I was out of that courtroom like a scalded cat. This called for a celebration, so I bought as much drink as I could afford and spent three whole glorious days in total oblivion. World War Three could have started and I wouldn't have known a thing about it. I was happily blind drunk. On the third night of my celebrations a police officer found me sitting in someone else's car singing at the top of my voice. He dragged me on to the road and ordered me to leave town there and then, otherwise I'd be locked up and face court charges for drunkenness. I took his advice and wobbled down the main road which led out of town.

I became a wanderer again. The judge's words were still ringing in my ears and I knew I couldn't return to my life of crime, so I turned to a life of drink instead. Being smashed out of my mind was quite good fun and it wasn't a criminal offence, so I took up my new alcoholic profession with gusto.

I decided to head back to London—Grandad had enjoyed a drunken existence on the Embankment and I decided to do the same. After a couple of weeks I looked like a tramp. My trousers and jacket were dirty and smelly, my shirt collar was black, my muddy shoes were down-at-heel and my face was covered in unshaven stubble. I must have looked twice my age, but I didn't care. When you lose your self-respect, you lose the ability to care. As the days turned to weeks, I lost everything except my desire for drink. I slept on newspapers like the other alcoholics on the Embankment. We seldom ate. What was the point of buying food when you could afford a bottle of methylated spirits and forget about the world? I was only twenty-two but it felt seventy-two.

I was also a heavy smoker. Cigarettes cost money, so I started picking up dog-ends from the pavements and rummaging in litter-bins to see if someone had accidentally thrown a whole cigarette away inside a packet. I used to put all my finds into a tin, scuttle on to a seat, tip out the tobacco and roll myself a smoke.

My existence wasn't an unhappy one. For most of the time I didn't have a care in the world and I was more than happy to be drunk for as many hours of the day as I could afford. People on the Embankment called me 'Laughing Peter' because I was always happy and joking. I would do anything for a drink—I've often sung and danced in a pub for the price of a short.

But occasionally I would surface to reality and see myself as I really was. At those times I hated looking in mirrors or shop windows because they showed me up for what I was—a dirty good-for-nothing, living from one drink to the next. Then I would bang my head against a wall in sheer frustration and bewilderment. 'Where are you going, Peter?' was the question that span around inside my head.

And I would reply: 'Nowhere.'

During that period I shuffled into several Salvation Army hostels where I saw men supposedly make a commitment to God. 'They're only doing it for a bed,' I used to think. I preferred to sleep rough.

5

A Brand-New 'New-Man'

I ended up in Manchester having hitch-hiked there from London. Little did I realize as the miles sped past, that the old Peter Newman was travelling to his death. I was to meet God in Manchester.

I've talked to a lot of people who have met God for themselves, and many have told me that, at different times in their lives, they have felt his presence. I hadn't told anybody, but I had too. I remember when I was a little boy in Sunday School. I wasn't allowed into the main hall but was taken upstairs where a man was on his knees crying and praying for me. I felt God in that room.

Then there was the fairground in Luton. I was working on the rides when suddenly I could hear the Salvation Army Band playing. I jumped off the Waltzer so that I could listen to the music which was drifting across the field. There was a warm, wonderful presence around me. I felt daft because I knew that I wanted to pray. Tears came into my eyes. I told the gaffer I was nipping off for five minutes and I ran across the field to where the band was playing. I followed them down the hill, rounded the corner with them—then dived into the first pub I came to. Try as

I might, I couldn't understand the peculiar feelings which had so gripped me.

Then there was the old Army Scripture reader in Benghazi who waited for me to return drunk to the barracks every night. I used to stagger into his room on his arm and he would help me sit down and get me to sing 'Guide me, O thou Great Jehovah' with him. I was drunk, but he was serious. I didn't ever let on to that old man, but every now and then, drunk though I was, I would feel that intangible Presence.

And here I was in Manchester, looking every inch a tramp, about to meet God properly at last. I knew there was a Salvation Army hostel in Francis Street and I made straight for it. Time and need had eroded my principles about staying in hostels. I was glad of any free hand-outs I could get, no matter what the source. Just as long as those too-good-to-be-true officers didn't start going on about the Lord and God and all that, I was quite happy to borrow one of their beds and wash the bad taste out of my mouth with some 'Sally Bash' tea.

Once installed in the hostel, I settled into my usual drinking routine. The nickname of 'Laughing Peter' wasn't particularly applicable at that time. I was starting to get really fed up with my alcoholic, filthy lifestyle and I'd long since been feeling that there had to be something else to life other than dog ends and booze. But what? I sat and chatted to one of the hostel officers one day, and asked him if joining the Salvation Army would make me any different.

'No,' he said, and I was shocked at his answer. Why then, I wondered, had they all shouted 'come and join us' so often and so long, if it wasn't going to change people? He must have seen my amazement because he looked at me and said: 'Peter, the only thing that could ever really change you and your life is a person-to-person meeting with the Lord Jesus Christ.'

My hackles rose straight away—which Christ would want to meet me person-to-person? I was dirty, smelly and had nothing to offer. Oh, it was all right for the young Army officer—he was all bright and shining and clean. So I retaliated in the best way I knew how—I swore loudly at him and told him where he could stuff his religion. He was persistent though and insisted that I should pray. I knew that the only way to get out of his clutches was to let him have his way, so he prayed. Then he got me to pray after him—I didn't know what I said at the time, but like a child I said whatever he said. Then I escaped into the nearest pub.

The next day I had a strange experience: I could not leave the hostel. We had two exits and every time I went to leave there was an invisible barrier that I couldn't break through. For several hours I walked around the hostel, failing to get out. Suddenly the Army officer who had prayed with me earlier approached me and said, 'Peter, do you want a job?'

To my utter amazement I heard myself reply, 'Yes', and I found myself cleaning the toilets in the hostel. My opinion of men who capitulated to become workers in hostels was that they had succumbed to the lowest form of employment; thieving and even begging were higher. My views were well known in the hostel, and many a man had felt the lashing of my tongue for stooping so low. The news soon spread. Those who thought they were in the know rumoured that my employment was just a ploy to enable me to rob the hostel.

As weeks went by I was given a cubicle to sleep in all to myself. If you knew anything about hostel hierarchy, you'd know that that was quite an achievement.

I thought long and deep about what the officer had said to me, although I didn't tell him, and one night I decided I would have a bash at praying. It was years since I'd last prayed by myself and I felt a bit ridiculous even thinking about it. But now I made up my mind—just so long as no one was going to overhear.

I stood on my bed and looked over the partition into the cubicle on the left. It was empty. Then I peered over into the one on the right. That too was empty. I was so determined that no one was going to know that Peter Newman had been praying that I put a chair under the door handle as an extra precaution. Feeling absolutely foolish, I dropped to my knees. Grandad had prayed on his knees and he knew God so I felt I should do the same. I took a deep breath and announced: 'God, I don't really believe you exist, but if you do, you've got to help me. You've got to stop me from drinking and if you do I'll serve you for the rest of my life. Amen.' I stuck the last bit on the end as a kind of deal just so there would be something in it for God—if he existed, that was.

I didn't tell a soul about my little prayer session and I got on with life in the hostel. Within a few weeks they promoted me to tea-boy. It was my job to serve the morning and afternoon teas and I got a nice, white jacket to do it in. All the other lads thought I'd wangled the job so I could make off with the takings.

I was serving teas out of the giant urn one Saturday morning when in walked an old pal of mine. Once upon a time he'd been a wealthy aristocratic sort of chap, but he'd fallen on hard times. He still had a very upper-class impression of himself and always reckoned he was a cut above the other riff-raff who frequented the hostels. Well, when he saw me serving up the tea he was absolutely amazed that Peter Newman, his friend, should be doing something so lowly and menial. 'Peter,' he said to me, 'how could you possibly do a job like this? Come,' he said, theatrically patting his pocket. 'I have money. Lots of it. Let's go out and enjoy ourselves.'

At once I slipped off my white jacket and left the queue of men with their tongues hanging out for a cuppa. I was away to share my old drinking companion's good fortune, wherever it had come from.

We marched into the nearest pub and he bought me a drink. I took one mouthful and thumped it back on to the bar. 'This tastes awful,' I said to him and complained to the barman.

'There's nothing wrong with my beer,' he said tetchily. 'Go somewhere else if you don't like it.' So we did, and it was the same story all over again. Try as I might, I just couldn't drink any alcohol because it tasted foul and smelled rotten. My friend, however, had no difficulty downing his liquid refreshment and by the time we'd visited half a dozen pubs, he was showing the first signs of alcoholic merriment.

We ended up in a hotel bar where we picked up a couple of women. I was sober as a judge and the more I looked at my drunken friend, the more irritated I became. To crown it all, one of the women was making eyes at me and I wasn't in the least bit interested.

'Here, Peter,' said my friend, waving a fiver dramatically under my nose, 'another round, my man.'

The women giggled as I obediently took the money and went to the bar to order the drinks. I picked up the tray and was returning to the cosy little drunken party when suddenly I thought: 'Peter, what on earth are you doing here?' Without a word of explanation, I was off.

I felt thoroughly miserable as I walked down the road towards the hostel. Things were bad—even drink tasted revolting, so what was there left to enjoy? I started to cry with despair. Then I heard my voice saying: 'God, I don't believe you exist; but *if* you do, you've got to help me.'

Then it dawned on me. God had made the drink taste so vile. God had helped me. God really did exist. Suddenly I felt clean, and free, as if a weight had been lifted from my shoulders. I jumped in the air, kicked my heels, then sped to the hostel. Only a few hours earlier I'd left a queue of thirsty men and headed out for a drunken binge, and here I was returning, talking excitedly about God. I ran straight towards the Major's room. I almost fell through the door with eagerness. 'Major,' I announced, 'I know there's a God. What do I do now?'

The Major looked up from his desk, somewhat surprised. 'If you know there's a God, go and read your Bible,' he said.

His answer wasn't quite what I expected. 'I'm not reading that rubbish,' I told him.

'Go and read the Bible and pray to the God you're talking about and he will show you the truth,' he said and put his head down to get on with his paperwork.

I left the room, ran up to my cubicle and rooted out the Bible which was stuffed in the back of my locker. I opened it. 'God,' I said, 'that man downstairs said that you would speak to me from this book. So I'm asking you to do it because I don't even know where to begin reading.'

I looked down to where the page was open and read these words: 'But as many as received him, to them gave he power to become the sons of God, even to them that believe on his name.'

Now, that made sense to me but I didn't know who 'he' was. 'So you'll have to tell me, God,' I said.

As I read on I discovered that 'he' was Jesus, and then I came to the bit which made me leap to my feet with excitement. 'He that comes unto me I will in no wise cast out.' That was me! Jesus accepted me, just as I was, mucky clothes and all, and he wasn't going to turn me away!

All I had in the world was a pair of Wimpey boots pinched from a building site, a pair of old grey flannels with the knees out, and a T-shirt. I didn't even have any socks or underwear to my name, but all of a sudden, I felt richer than a millionaire. I had found him, the pearl of great price. I was his son. He had claimed me and made me his own. I can't begin to describe the joy I felt at my discovery—I felt as if I belonged to someone who cared for me deeply and that I was no longer left to struggle through the mish-mash of life alone. I had a Shepherd, a Saviour and, most of all, a Friend.

I had entered a new world. It was like being reborn. The grass was greener, the sky was bluer, birds were singing, people were people. I was a new creation, a brand-new 'new-man'.

There were some anxious moments, too. I wondered whether it would last, whether I was dreaming. There was plenty around to feed my doubts. People were bewildered; some became angry and frustrated; others amazed. Some reactions were violent and taunts and threats were commonplace.

But thank God there were others who knew the same Jesus as Saviour. They encouraged me to trust the written word of God, and they trusted God with me.

6

A Way of Escape

The Major called me into his office. 'Peter,' he said, looking up from his big wooden desk, 'I want you to take the hostel takings to the bank for me, please.'

I stared at him in disbelief. There were over four hundred beds in that hostel and that added up to an awful lot of money. This had to be some kind of joke.

'Er, you're just havin' me on, Sir,' I said to him, 'because I ain't ever been in a bank before in my life and I just wouldn't know what to do.' Well, I made that my excuse anyway. The real reason for my hesitation was that I didn't trust myself with all those pound notes—didn't the Major know that in times past I would have cheerfully nicked a pair of wings from an angel without even a twinge of remorse? Now, being a hostel foreman (my new position) was one thing, but trusting me with hundreds of pounds was another. It was out of the question.

The Major, however, didn't share my point of view. He thrust the cash bag and the paying book at me, told me to hand it all over to the cashier in the bank, then stood up to see me to the door. I was fuming. I turned to him on the steps of the hostel and said accusingly: 'Major, you do realize what you're doing, don't you?'

'Yes, I know exactly what I'm doing, Peter. Now get a move on or else the bank'll be closed before you even get there,' and in he marched leaving me grasping the blue bank bag. I stepped on to the street feeling absolutely livid—the Major was deliberately giving me the chance to take his money—and it was very likely that I would take him up on his offer. There was I, trying to lead a good, straight Christian life, and all he could do to help was to thrust temptation into my hands. I headed dismally up the road. The bank was only five hundred yards away, but it felt like five hundred miles. I watched the buses as they roared past me. 'Now that one would take me out of Manchester,' I said to myself but before I could continue my little mental dialogue, a very strange thing happened. My feet broke into a run and I sped post haste to the bank. I almost fell through the door before throwing the bag and paying-in book at the cashier. 'Here,' I said, 'cop this little lot.' He gave me a strange look and then started counting the cash and marking up the book.

He handed the empty bag and the book back to me and I stormed out of the bank towards the hostel. I knew that God had taken a hold of my feet and had caused me to run to the bank before I could do anything silly like making off with the money, but I wasn't angry with him. No, it was the Major I was angry with—he'd been the one to put temptation across the path and I was jolly well going to give him a big piece of my mind. I raced up the hostel steps and barged into his office without even knocking at the door.

'Here,' I said, throwing the book and the bag on to his desk, 'and don't you ever do that again. You knew I'd think about making off with it all—and a right mess I'd be in now if I had.'

I don't know what I expected him to do, but smiling wasn't on my list of guesses. He stood up and walked round his desk and put his arm on my shoulder.

'Peter,' he said, 'I had to trust God just as you did. I've been let down more times than I care to remember but I had to give you the chance to prove something for yourself. Something very important happened to you today—now off you go and just think about it.'

Well, I felt the wind drain out of my sails. All the anger I'd felt just disappeared as I turned round and meekly went out of his office and up to my cubicle. I sat on my bed and thought about what he'd said. Something important, he'd told me. Well, yes, God had helped me resist a temptation which would have destroyed me, once upon a time. He'd made a way of escape for me. I reckon he knew that I didn't really want to walk out of his will by doing something dishonest, so he made my feet move a little faster than normal. Yes, I thought to myself, I've learned that sin and the old ways don't have to rule you when you're saved. In the old days it was almost as if I couldn't help but do wrong, but things were different now. I really was a new person.

I remember the thrill of getting my first week's pay at the hostel. It had been years since I'd done an honest day's work and it felt good to pick up my little pay cheque from the hostel office. I'd earned the grand sum of 13/- (65p) and as soon as I got it, I took the bus into Salford where I marched into a second-hand clothes shop. A man and a woman were standing behind the counter.

'Now listen,' I said, closing the door behind me. 'I've got thirteen bob and need to be rigged out. These are all the clothes I've got,' I said, pointing at my dirty old suit, 'so what can you do for me, guvnor? You see, this is the story. Jesus has done something for me. You see how dirty and tatty my clothes are—well, I used to be like that on the inside as well but Jesus has cleaned me up...' And on I went for the next quarter of an hour. I gave them my testimony and didn't miss anything out.

When I finished, the man spoke up. 'I'm a Methodist,' he said, his voice trembling. 'I haven't been to church in years but I'm definitely going this Sunday. I'd almost forgotten that God is real.'

The woman spoke up next. 'What about me?' she said. 'I'm a Roman Catholic but I've never heard anything like this before. I want to be like you.'

But I never had the sense or wisdom to lead them to the Lord. I started to explain why I only had 13/- to spend on my new wardrobe. 'So what have you got that'll fit me?' I asked them. Well, I came out of that shop kitted up with everything I needed, from shoes to vests. They even gave me some free shaving gear and I said goodbye to them feeling richer than a king.

Life at the hostel was running smoothly but I started to feel unsettled. God was ready to move me on.

7

Something New and Clean

The new digs I moved into weren't very grand. I had an upstairs room in a terraced house in Manchester. It had a bed, a small wardrobe, a dressing table and fading wallpaper, but it was my first real step into independence. I also had a job—in an iron foundry. The men I worked with gave me a hard time because they couldn't understand me and the more I tried to explain about my new life, the worse the misunderstanding. They thought I was a bit mad and, looking back, I suppose I can appreciate why.

My new digs weren't far from the Salvation Army hall and to get to the Sunday services I had to walk past two pubs that I had once frequented. If I wanted to avoid walking past them, I had to make a lengthy detour round the backstreets, so on my first visit to the hall since moving, I decided to take the most direct route. My Bible presented me with quite a problem—it was big and black and wouldn't fit inside any of my pockets, but I was loth to carry it ostentatiously under my arm to advertise my conversion to all my old drinking mates. Wisdom, I said to myself, is the order of the day. I rammed it inside my raincoat and headed off to the service.

It was too early for the pubs to open so I got to the hall without meeting up with any of my old companions, but I knew the story would be different on the journey home. After the service I again rammed my Bible inside my raincoat. 'Peter,' the Major said to me, watching my antics, 'you're taking the easy way out.'

'Oh, am I now?' I said, rising to the challenge. 'Well, Peter Newman never takes the easy way out.' And with that I marched out of the hall with my Bible clenched firmly in my hand.

I was walking past one of the pubs when the landlady came out, followed by a band of faithfuls. She saw me straight away and shouted: 'Hey, Peter, come on in and have a drink. We've missed you—you weren't really all that bad you know.' Then all the lads around her started laughing and shouting 'Hallelujah!' I hardly dared look in their direction—I kept my eyes straight ahead and continued walking.

The same thing happened week after week. The landlady and her mates knew what time I'd be coming back from church and they would line up on the pavement and wait for me. It only took a few minutes to run the gauntlet past them, but they were the longest moments of the week. My big black Bible seemed to weigh a ton as I scuttled along, deliberately keeping my eyes fixed in the direction I was going. Home was always a welcome sight, and many's the time I'd rush up the stairs, throw my Bible down and fall onto my bed absolutely breathless.

I knew that they could never persuade me to go back to my old ways—drinking and Peter Newman had parted company for good. My fear was that I might lash out and give them a belt round the jaws. The old Peter Newman was a violent man, and while I had learned to trust God for many things, I wasn't totally convinced that the old aggro had disappeared. I'm glad to say that I survived my Sunday ordeals without putting any of my old drinking pals in hospital. After a couple of months the novelty of goading me seemed to wear off and they eventually stopped waiting for me to walk past the pub.

I used every opportunity I could find to preach the gospel. I soon discovered the secret of preaching in open-air meetings—I would direct my voice towards a wall which acted as an amplifier so that the afternoon rest of even more people was disturbed. If I had to travel anywhere by bus, I would stand on my feet on the open top deck and start to give my testimony. Not everyone appreciated my zeal and I was told to sit down and shut up on more than one occasion.

Someone once made the dreadful mistake of giving me an old drum. I used to take it on to the streets and bang it as loudly as I could. I couldn't drum properly but everyone knew I was there and they would come out to find out what all the racket was about. As soon as I had an attentive, curious audience, I would introduce myself and tell them what Jesus had done for me.

I've spent many a night selling War Cry magazines in the pubs of Manchester. When other people sold the magazine they would tap possible buyers on the shoulder, look at them pleadingly and rattle their collection tins, but I had a better selling technique. I used to stand on a table and sing 'The Old Rugged Cross'. I sold far more copies than anyone else. I still can't decide if the men were genuinely moved or if they bought my wares to shut me up.

I once went back to my home town to preach outside a pub I had been drunk in many times. I was in the middle of telling the assembled crowd how the police had thrown me out of the town, telling me never to return, when that very sergeant rounded the corner. 'And if you don't believe me,' I shouted, pointing to the poor bobby, 'then ask him.' Well, he was off like a shot, much to the amusement of my little congregation.

The pub landlord had been sitting in his bedroom listening to me. As I was getting ready to return to Manchester, he came over, looking quite tearful. 'Peter,' he said, 'I'm just amazed at what's happening to you. You're a different lad from the one I remember. If ever you need money for your work, just ask me and I'll give it to you.' I felt humbled at this—years before he used to loan me money for drink and now he wanted to give me money to help spread the gospel.

I was often puzzled and hurt at the way people reacted to me. I was only a very young Christian and I just naturally assumed that churchgoers knew Jesus like I knew him. I remember standing on the steps of one very posh church and saying 'Praise the Lord' to the people as they walked in. They just glanced at me as if I was daft. 'Poor soul,' their looks seemed to say.

But even those icy stares could not freeze the new life which was bubbling up inside me. I was full of the joy of the Lord. I may not have known much about social graces but I knew about God's grace. I knew that he loved and saved the outcast and that he could make something new and clean out of something dirty. I knew that he loved the unlovely, that his hand could reach down into the blackest cave of despair and pull the captive out of the darkness and into his most marvellous light. I knew all these things, not from reading a book, but because they had happened to me.

8

A Flock of Sheep to Preach to

I walked wearily upstairs to my room. That day at the foundry had seemed particularly hard and all I wanted to do was go to bed and sleep. My usual nightly routine was to pray and read my Bible but that night, for the first time since getting saved, I just went straight off to sleep.

I awoke with a start just before four o'clock in the morning. The alarm hadn't gone off so I couldn't understand why I was awake. The rest of the house was silent. I looked around the room, wondering what had woken me from such a deep sleep. As I turned my head to the left, I saw the face of Jesus. My heart started to beat so loudly that I was sure everyone in the house would hear it. I was captivated by his eyes—they were so beautiful yet they seemed so sad. I immediately felt sorry for not praying and talking to him before going off to sleep. My eyes moved slowly from his and I started to look at the rest of his face. There were some long thorns sticking into his forehead and some blood was slowly trickling down his cheekbone.

When I saw his blood, I was completely overtaken by a feeling of awe. I knew that that blood had been shed for me and the realization of his love and his majesty drove me from my bed and on to the floor where I lay face down, hardly daring to move. The presence of God was almost overpowering. I felt so small, so worthless, so insignificant. I looked up to see if his face was still there. It wasn't, but the power of God's presence was as real as ever.

Then I heard his voice. 'Peter,' he said, 'I have called you to be an evangelist.' Then the consciousness of his presence went.

I can't remember how long I lay on the floor before climbing, dazed, back into bed. As soon as my head touched the pillow, I fell into the deep sleep I'd wakened from.

As soon as I woke up, memories of the visitation flooded back to me. I knew I hadn't dreamt the whole thing. The word evangelist seemed to be burning in my heart. But there was a problem—I hadn't a clue what an evangelist was or what he did. My knowledge of the Bible was still very limited and big words always flummoxed me. I looked the word up in my concordance and I soon discovered that Philip had been an evangelist. So the matter was settled. I was going to be like Philip.

It was several days before I told anyone about what had happened to me that night. The first person to know was an officer at the Salvation Army. He decided that I might be officer material and that I ought to start the candidates' course. One of the main problems was my lack of basic education. I could just about read and write but that was all. A kind Salvation Army couple volunteered to teach me the basics of English and I was thrilled to discover the difference between nouns, verbs and adjectives and the like. I worked hard to acquire these new skills, and when the big day of the interview arrived, I felt that I stood a fairly good chance of being accepted.

There were quite a few candidates waiting to be interviewed by the selection panel. When it was my turn, I was taken into a room where the members of the panel were sitting and I remember thinking that they all looked like saints. As I stood before them, all I could hear was a voice ringing in my ears: 'Peter, I have called you to be an evangelist.'

'Excuse me,' I said, before they had a chance to start questioning me, 'can you guarantee that I'll be an evangelist?' They all looked a bit startled at my uninvited question but after a few seconds an elderly gentleman, who had just finished reading my report, muttered something about my past experiences being invaluable in the social work side of the Army.

'Sirs,' I insisted, hardly hearing what the gentleman had said, 'you must guarantee that I'm to be an evangelist.'

The panel asked me what I meant and I explained as best as I could. 'So you see,' I said, 'I've got to be like him in the Bible.'

'Like who in the Bible?' said the old gentleman.

'Like Philip,' I said, exasperated by their lack of understanding. They all looked at each other, thanked me very much for attending the interview, then told me I could go. That was the last I heard from them. I wasn't too upset about not being accepted. After all, if they couldn't guarantee that I would be working as an evangelist, then that settled the matter as far as I was concerned. I may have been a bit thick academically, but at least I knew that I had to be obedient to what God had shown me.

Before the interview I'd been so sure that I would be an officer that I'd handed in my notice at the foundry. So with no job to keep me in Manchester, I decided to spend Christmas with my sister. I tried to get a job in the area but everyone remembered me as the pre-converted Peter. I bought a bike, a bucket and some ladders and set myself up in business as a window cleaner. I used to go from house to house, singing at the top of my voice and giving my testimony whenever I could.

Most of my spare time was spent up in the hills. I loved the countryside and spent most evenings and weekends stalking across the fields preaching to the turnips. On a really good day I would have a flock of sheep to preach to. They might not have been a responsive congregation, but they looked as if they were listening to me and at least I was practising at being an evangelist.

On Sundays I went to the local Baptist church to worship. One week a retired missionary, who must have been well into his eighties, was preaching. His text was 'Thou art the man' and in the middle of his sermon he stepped down from his pulpit, walked down the aisle and stood in front of me. He announced: 'And thou art the man, Peter, to preach next Sunday.' I could hardly believe my ears; I was panic-stricken. But I wasn't one to back out. I had wanted to move forward—and here I was, graduating from turnips, to sheep, to people. The missionary packed me off home with a commentary on Luke's Gospel which I duly devoured over the following days.

The big day arrived. We all sang some hymns, listened to the Bible readings and then I got to my feet and strode to the pulpit. I delivered my sermon and sat down, eager for the service to end so that I could ask the old missionary how I'd sounded.

'That was marvellous, Peter,' he said with a twinkle in his eye. 'It's the first time I've heard three sermons preached inside of twenty minutes. Well done!'

It was the beginning of small things. I was asked to preach again, so my sermon can't have been all that bad, and then I was invited to preach in a nearby church. This is it, I thought; my fame is spreading. I was so thrilled at being so much in demand that I persuaded my step-sister, Shirley, to come along and listen to me spout forth. She agreed to come.

The Sunday arrived. I had my sermon all ready and I was delighted that Shirley was going to hear what a good preacher I was. We arrived at the church where I was to lead the hymn singing as well as deliver my pearls of scriptural wisdom. I climbed ceremoniously into the pulpit and eyed the congregation. The church wasn't exactly filled to capacity. In its heyday it had seated six hundred. That particular Sunday it boasted a congregation of six, including Shirley and the organist. But I was undaunted.

I handed the organist the list of hymns which I'd chosen to fit in with my sermon.

'I can't play any of these,' she whispered as she scanned the titles.

'Well,' I whispered back, 'what can you play then?'

She was thoughtful for a second. 'How about "All Things Bright and Beautiful"?' she replied.

So 'All Things Bright and Beautiful' it was, although the singing hardly did justice to the title. The hymn ended and I opened my Bible to start preaching. This was the moment I'd dreamed about all week—Shirley was sure to tell everyone how inspired my preaching was and how the call of God was unmistakably on my life. I took a deep breath and was about to start when the church doors opened at the back and a man called out: 'Come down, young man, I'm booked to preach here today.'

I could hardly believe my ears. He strode down to the front and stood at the pulpit steps waiting for me to climb down and make way for him. I felt so humiliated that I wished the ground would open and swallow me up. I glanced at Shirley on the front row. Surprise was written right across her face. I picked up my Bible, walked down the steps, passed the preacher and sat down next to Shirley. I haven't a clue what he preached about. I was too angry and upset to care. My moment of glory had been snatched away from me and now Shirley might never know how brilliant a preacher I was. I didn't even have the grace to say goodbye to the preacher after the service. I just wanted to be as far away from that place of defeat as quickly as possible.

It was some time later that God showed me why he had allowed such a humiliating thing to happen. He wanted all the glory, and I had to remember that I was only his vessel. He was the treasure within me and I had no right to seek after fame or self-glorification. The incident also taught me that you should never try to impress men—God is the one we should seek to serve and to please. So what my step-sister thought or thinks about me and my preaching is quite irrelevant. These are lessons which God has had to teach me over and over again, and the lessons aren't all learnt yet.

A few weeks after my demise, someone asked if I wanted to go to a nearby town to hear an evangelist who was holding some meetings. My ears pricked up at the word evangelist and I agreed. I went the first night and was so impressed by his preaching that I went back every other night too. Only one thing troubled me and that was his suits. They were—well—almost theatrical, with gold threads one night and silver ones the next. If I was to be an evangelist, then I decided that God would have to make a special set of rules for me because nothing on earth would induce me to wear such gaudy clothes.

This evangelist chap fascinated me. I wanted to find out as much about him as I could. I wanted to see how he lived, how he spoke to people when he was off the platform, what he ate, how he behaved. So I gave up window cleaning for the week, found the hotel he was staying in and started to spy on him. I was there when he turned up for breakfast. I was there at lunch-time too. I watched his every move and was quick to discover something about him which disturbed me deeply: he was suave and well polished. I noted that he probably knew the difference between an adjective and a verb without being told.

9

Never the Same Again

So the great evangelist came and went and my life settled back into its usual routine of window cleaning, walking in the hills and preaching in local churches. The days ran into weeks, the weeks into months.

One day my sister asked me if I'd ever thought of getting married. I said that I felt marriage was not for me and that my eye was on the call of God. In my own wisdom I felt that marriage would be a hindrance. Perhaps my subconscious reminded me of the anger of that minister's wife when he had tried to help me. I headed for town to keep an appointment with some dirty windows.

I reached the traffic lights as they turned green and was about to drive on when a Salvation Army officer rode straight across my path on her bicycle while her lights were on red. She was in full uniform, bonnet and all and she had a little dog in the basket in front of the handlebars. She was pedalling with such concentration that she didn't even notice me brake to avoid hitting her.

'Typical,' I thought, 'just because she's in the

Army she thinks she can do anything and go anywhere. It's a good thing God's got his hand on her, otherwise she'd be splattered across the bonnet of my car by now.' I was in the middle of mentally giving her a piece of my mind when something seemed to go 'ping'. 'Cupid' had shot the arrow. Then God spoke to me. 'That's the girl you're going to marry, Peter,' he said. 'I've chosen her for you.'

Without losing a second, I changed direction and set off to find out where she lived. I could hardly let the girl I was going to marry pedal out of my life before she had properly pedalled into it. I drove up one street, then another, and then I saw her Salvation Army bonnet bobbing up and down. I followed behind and watched her turn into a side street. She got off her bike and went into a house. I got out of my car, made some inquiries and discovered it was the Salvation Army officers' quarters. Straight away I felt very led to clean their windows for them. When I finished I knocked on the door. The girl on the bike answered it and we soon got chatting. I discovered she was called Barbara.

I floated home on air. 'I've met the girl I'm going to marry,' I said to my sister as soon as I opened the front door. She seemed confused. 'But I thought you weren't going to get married,' she said, 'and anyway, does this girl know you're going to marry her? It all seems mighty quick to me.'

'No, she doesn't know yet,' I answered. 'I only met her today.'

'Goodness me, Peter,' said my sister as she sank into a chair. 'You really are the limit, you know. You can't just marry the girl without letting her know about it first. You want to get some of these silly ideas out of your head. If you're going to marry this whatever-she's-called, then you're going to have to court her and take her out like any other normal young man. You can't just meet her one day and wed her the next. Honestly, I sometimes wonder what sort of religion you've got!'

I smiled at her and went to unload the car. She was perfectly right, of course, so I decided to ride over to the house and ask Barbara out. She said yes and our courtship began. We had a lot in common but the most important thing was that we both wanted God's will for our lives and we both wanted to serve him. We both prayed about our relationship and exactly six months from the day God spoke to me and said she was to be my wife, we were married. The only sad part was that Barbara had to leave the Salvation Army because I wasn't even a member, never mind an officer. She decided to make a clean break, which was not pleasant for either her or the Army, but it had to be.

After the wedding we went to live in Barbara's home town of Plymouth. We moved into a flat, attended a Salvation Army hall on Sundays but spent Saturday nights in a little evangelical mission hall. Within months I was preaching all over the place—I was on the Methodist plan and the Baptist and Congregationalist list of speakers. I preached three times on a Sunday and worked hard on a building site during the week.

Bit by bit we started getting a home together. On

the surface, everything seemed to be working out well. After a year we had our first little girl, Elaine, and I should have been the happiest man around. But I had a deep sense of frustration. The call of God, which had once so burned in my heart, had somehow been swamped by the pressures of building a home, supporting a family and becoming a prolific preacher. My days were full of activity but somehow I felt there was something important missing.

It was a few months before I found out what it was. Meanwhile I was offered a job which I'd always wanted. I was to be a sales representative. No longer would I need overalls, dungarees and clodhopper boots. I was to have a respectable white-collar job. My hands would be nice and clean when I got home at night—I would no longer have to spend a quarter of an hour scrubbing the muck from them before cuddling my young daughter.

So each morning, I left home wearing a smart suit and brandishing a briefcase, the ultimate symbol of my new found success. I earned good money and our future was bright.

I was still a popular preacher. One week Barbara and I were asked to take some evening meetings in a mission hall. Each evening I rushed home from work, grabbed some tea, then bundled myself, Barbara and little Elaine into the car to drive to the little hall where Barbara would sing and I would preach. It was to be a week which would change my whole Christian life.

The beginning of new things started the night we gave a man a lift home. As we drove along he turned to me and said: 'Peter, you need the baptism in the Holy Spirit!'

The baptism in the Holy Spirit? How dare he suggest that I wasn't properly saved! I was very annoyed at his impertinence—how could he talk to me, a preacher, in such a way? Who did he think he was?

I think he sensed my disapproval because he immediately started to explain that this baptism in the Holy Spirit was a separate experience to salvation and that it had given the early disciples the power to witness and to evangelize.

Now I was interested.

As soon as we got home I opened my Bible and read about the promise of the Comforter in St John's Gospel. Then I turned to the Acts of the Apostles. I'd studied it thousands of times before, yet it was as if I was reading it for the first time. I read about the gift of tongues and other gifts of this Holy Spirit.

I set off in hot pursuit of the subject. I talked about it with Christians from many different denominations and was often surprised at the reaction it brought. Some told me to keep well away from such teaching. They said that surely I realized that the baptism in the Holy Spirit had been for the early church only, and that God was doing things differently now. I discovered that the gift of tongues was a great bone of contention. Some people told me it was from the devil and that I should steer clear of it at all costs. Others I spoke to were far more sympathetic and said that, while they themselves hadn't experienced the baptism in the Holy Spirit, they felt it was a valid experience for the church today. Looking back, I feel a bit sorry for Barbara. All I ever seemed to talk to her about over those weeks was the baptism in the Holy Spirit. She showed an interest in what I said, but she didn't share my insatiable appetite for the subject.

The man who first told me about it got in touch with me and asked me over to his house for tea. I eagerly accepted his invitation and drove to his home with a great feeling of anticipation. 'Lord,' I prayed as I drove along, 'if this experience is for me, then could I have it tonight, please?'

We had our tea, talked about the week's meetings I'd taken in the little mission hall, discussed the state of the world and the Christian church, but we never seemed to get round to talking about the one thing I was desperate to hear about. He kept getting up and down to put records on and I thought, 'Lord, isn't he ever going to get on with it and tell me all he knows about the baptism in the Spirit?'

After what seemed like a decade he asked me if I would like to pray with him. We went to his bedroom where we would not be disturbed, and at once he began to pray. By now I was feeling totally exasperated. My mind was full of all sorts of things, but it eventually started to tune in with God. I was praying quietly when I suddenly remembered the scripture which says that if you ask God for the Holy Spirit, then God will give him to you; he won't give you a stone instead.

'Lord,' I prayed silently, 'I only want what you have for me. I don't want anything else. . . .' And then it happened. I was miraculously and, in my case, dramatically baptized in the Holy Spirit. The only person I was aware of in that room was God. He was everywhere. I felt that I was being swept along on a tidal wave of his love and power. I don't know how many minutes ticked by, but I remember coming to and being somewhat surprised to find myself jumping up and down on this dear man's bed with my shoes on. I was singing and dancing and praising the Lord in a new language which just kept flowing out from my lips.

I told Barbara all about it when I eventually got home. She didn't say much, but she couldn't deny that something very extraordinary had happened to me. For three whole days I was 'drunk' in the Spirit. Every morning I left the house in my sober suit with my briefcase tightly clasped in my hand but, if anyone stopped to say hello, I could only say, 'Hallelujah!' and continue on my way singing and praising God. A week later the man who had prayed with me came to our house and prayed for Barbara and she too received the baptism of the Holy Spirit.

We were both quickened by the Spirit of God. It's little wonder that the devil has so many people blinded about the necessity of being baptized in the Spirit. It's like dynamite—once you receive it, you're never the same again. The Holy Spirit causes you to thirst and hunger after more of God. Barbara and I found that all we wanted to do was lay our lives unquestioningly before him. We asked him to do whatever he wanted with our lives. We were willing to go where he wanted us to go; to speak what he gave us to say. We entered a new realm of yielding. We both felt his presence in a way which we'd never done before. After all those barren, dry months it was as refreshing as the rain itself. The wilderness which had sprung up in our hearts was indeed starting to blossom as a rose. God became our main topic of conversation—we couldn't help but praise him for leading us into this new experience.

We talked eagerly of going to Bible College. We knew it would be a big step, but we were open to whatever the Lord had for us, and Bible College seemed the logical step. But God doesn't work according to our own understanding. One evening, when we were both praying quietly in tongues, I felt God start to give me the interpretation.

Neither of us knew much about the gifts of the Holy Spirit, but what we know in our heads isn't always important in the kingdom of God. Obedience is the key to blessing. God gave me a chapter and a verse to look up in the Bible. I eagerly turned to 1 John 2 verse 27 and read: 'But the anointing which ye have received of him abideth in you, and ye need not that any man teach you: but... the same anointing teacheth you of all things.' We knew straight away that God was telling us that Bible College was not going to be our next stopping place. We said amen to the will of God. We knew that if college was out, then he had something else in store for us. It still amazes me to think that God has a perfect plan for individual lives. All we need to do is to tune into him and wait on him and he will show us the way.

We were acknowledging him in all our ways, so he was bound by his word to direct our paths.

10

'I Can't Tell Them That!'

We were going to live in a Christian commune in Worthing. I resigned from my job; we found homes for all the much-loved bits and pieces of furniture we'd gathered together over our short married life. I felt I was responding to God who had spoken to me so clearly and said: 'Peter, leave all and follow me.'

The week before we were due to join the Christian Publicity Organisation Commune, I was booked to take a week's meetings. It was during that mission that God taught me a very big lesson, namely that we have to be wholly true before him and before our brothers and sisters in the Lord.

My wife was singing on the platform. The little church was packed to the doors. Barbara sounded beautiful and I was just sitting back drinking it all in when God spoke to me. 'Peter,' he said, 'what sort of picture of you and Barbara are you painting for all those people? Do they see you as the perfect young couple about to be launched out into the work of God? Peter, there are people here tonight who look at you both and feel so inadequate—they feel failures in comparison. There are married couples here who feel guilty because they have so many ups and downs in their home life. I want you to be truthful and to tell them exactly what happened before you both came to the meeting tonight.'

I held my breath. 'But God,' I argued, 'I can't tell them that. Barbara will have a fit and besides, it's personal!' But God had spoken and I had to bow to what he had told me to do. Barbara ended her song and I stood up, knowing very well that she would lynch me when we got home.

'Isn't my wife lovely?' I said to the congregation. 'Hasn't she got a lovely voice?' They all sat there smiling and nodded their heads.

'Aren't we a nice young couple, called of God, about to go into full-time work for him, going forth to conquer in his name?' And again they all sat nodding their heads in agreement.

'Well, let me tell you something which might surprise you all.' I glanced across at Barbara who was on the edge of her seat, looking alarmed. 'Before my wife and I came to the meeting tonight we had a humdinger of a row.' Barbara blanched, then she gasped, then she stared unbelievingly at me. The congregation followed suit, their eyes darting first to me then to her, then back to me again. I immediately started to preach.

Jesus says that you shall know the truth and the truth shall set you free. Many couples were set free that night. The enemy had had them bound with chains of condemnation. Why, they'd never dreamt that evangelists were just ordinary human beings who did such unspiritual things as row with their wives. I always feel it's very wrong of men of God to pretend to be what they aren't. So often they give the impression of being so perfect and they hate people to discover otherwise. Well, I love exposing the myth. Yes, evangelists are called of God, but they are no different from anybody else.

Jesus said that the greatest among you should minister to others. We all have a part to play in the body of Christ. An evangelist is called to preach the gospel, a prayer warrior is called to pray, someone given to hospitality is to open their home to others. We all have something to do in the kingdom of God and we should never puff ourselves up in the ministry which God has given to us.

So Barbara and I set off for Worthing with only our clothes, the baby's cot, our train tickets and a ten shilling note (fifty pence). We climbed into the carriage and settled in a compartment opposite two elderly ladies. Within hours of setting off in this new life of faith God showed us again that he is able to meet our needs.

We were all sitting there, gazing out of the windows at the countryside as it sped past us, when God spoke to me and told me to go to the dining car. 'But Lord,' I argued, 'I haven't got any money, especially if we're both supposed to go.' So I decided the Lord was only meaning me.

'No,' he said, 'take Barbara and go to the dining car.'

'But what about the baby, Lord?' I argued, still trying to wriggle out of it.

Just then one of the old ladies spoke up: 'If you two want to go and have some lunch, we'd be more than willing to look after the baby for you.'

'Thank you very much,' I said, with very mixed emotions. I told Barbara to hand Elaine over to them. Then I took her by the arm and led her into the corridor. There was a look of horror on her face. As soon as we were out of earshot she whispered, 'Where on earth are we going?' I said that God had spoken to me, that we should both go to the dining car.

'But we can't afford to. How much money have we got?' She knew full well what the answer was going to be and she looked exasperated when I waved the ten shilling note in the air. 'But we can't both have a meal with that,' she said. Now, she knew that I knew that, but God apparently didn't. 'God's spoken to me and we've got to do exactly what he says from now on,' I said and off we marched into the dining car.

When we came to our table my wife very wisely put me on the inside nearest the window, so she could sit near the aisle to make a quick getaway! The menu was brought to us. It was ten shillings and six pence each. We ordered two meals while I sat and nervously fingered the ten shilling note in my trouser pocket. It was round about election time and the man sitting opposite me started talking about the political climate of the day. This was my chance! I gradually turned the conversation round to the Lord and explained that one day the government of the world would be on his shoulders. The man seemed really interested and said I reminded him of someone he'd known who believed the same sort of things as we did. It transpired that I knew his friend and that we'd held open-air meetings together some years before.

We chatted merrily away, thoroughly enjoying the meal and the company of this stranger. Just after the ice-cream course my wife excused herself and said she had to go to see to the baby. What a wise woman she is! The cheese-board arrived next. I took a piece and was eating it with some celery, thinking 'This is the life,' when I remembered that at any minute the waiter was going to arrive with the bill. I stopped hearing what the man opposite me was saying. Panic started to well up from where my nice three-course meal was lying. Out of the corner of my eye I saw the waiter heading menacingly in my direction, holding a slip of paper in his hand. My heart was rattling against my rib-cage as, sure enough, he arrived and put the bill on a plate before me. As I reached out for it the man opposite me barred my arm, grabbed the piece of paper and said he would like to pay for our meal. I didn't argue with his kindness.

When I got back to the compartment I quietly told Barbara what had happened and we both simply sat there, praising the Lord in our hearts. It had seemed like a close shave, but we were both beginning to learn that God is often a God of the last minute. Just when it seems that all is lost, he makes a way where there wasn't one.

We've had hard times since and we've even wondered if God has forsaken and forgotten us, but always, just in the nick of time, he has met our need. I remember once living off a bag of wholemeal flour for days and days on end. We fried that flour, baked it, boiled it. We loved it, we hated it, we refused to eat it, then did so—because we were hungry.

We've had miracles of provision where groceries have literally turned up on our doorstep. God is a good God but we often don't discover his faithfulness until we launch out into the deep, cast out our nets and just wait to see him fill them.

11

God Answers Prayers

It was with great excitement and expectancy that we arrived at the old rectory which was to be our home in Worthing. The rambling old house had been acquired by the Christian Publicity Organisation some time before, but there was still quite a lot of work to be done on it. So I spent quite a lot of time helping to dig drains and do other plumbing work.

We were given a set of rooms to live in. There were about sixteen other people living in the house and I soon discovered why God had brought us to live in a commune. Living with a group of people isn't very easy. We're all different, we all have different personalities and quirks of character. More often than not we think it's the other fellow who's wrong and that God really ought to do a work in his heart, but all the time God is asking us to look at ourselves first. Living in close daily contact with others reveals what's in our own hearts and lives. I remember once hearing it said that if someone rubs you up the wrong way, then you're the one at fault because you shouldn't have a wrong way to be rubbed up! Well,

God took us to Worthing to teach us a few lessons. Looking back, I don't feel that we contributed much to the spiritual life of the commune—but it was good training ground for our souls!

As soon as we arrived, we were introduced to the other members of the household. I was to be one of two full-time evangelists and as soon as I met the other one, I knew I couldn't stand him. The feeling seemed to be mutual—we just couldn't get along together. Whether it was jealousy or plain strife, I don't know, but my heart sank when I discovered that we were expected to minister together and do our share of drain-digging together, too. Something about the man irritated me beyond measure. I knew the scriptures about loving one another but I couldn't bring myself to do it.

So there was I, the anointed, spiritual evangelist, seething because this other fellow even existed. As far as I was concerned, he was pig-headed, unteachable and unbearable. The fault lay entirely at his door—Peter Newman, I told myself, could get along with anyone and everyone, and if he couldn't, then the other chap was to blame.

Once the seeds of strife were sown, an evil root started to grow. My dislike for him became like a cancer which constantly ate away my peace and my joy. His face was before me when I woke in the morning and when I went to bed at night.

I lived in fear of the day when we would have to go out and minister the gospel together. I knew that the Spirit of God, gentle dove that he is, couldn't possibly flow between us: the resentment and dislike would put him to flight in an instant.

The problem came to a head within a few weeks. It was about four in the morning and I was unable to sleep. Barbara was out for the count so I decided to go downstairs and pray about the whole messy situation. I went into the empty living room and sank wearily to my knees. 'Lord,' I cried in desperation, 'what should I do?' I had hardly got the words out of my mouth when the door opened and in walked the man I was praying about. My heart sank to my knees.

'What are you doing up this time of night?' I asked him.

'I was wondering the same thing about you,' he replied. 'Tell me what you're up to.'

The moment of truth had come. 'I'm here talking to God about you,' I said. 'I'm afraid I just can't seem to get on with you at all.' I waited with bated breath for his reply.

'Well,' he said, 'what a coincidence. I've come downstairs to talk to God about you because I can't seem to get on with you either.'

We both began to laugh. Then we cried. Then we hugged each other and began to praise the Lord. The invisible barrier which had separated us had completely melted away. God taught us both a few lessons that night. First, that we have to bring our differences to one another as well as to him. Secondly, that the devil loves us to keep resentments and bitternesses to ourselves. He hates us to bring them into the light where they can be exposed for what they are. If they go unheeded, they fester in the dark recesses of our hearts and minds until one day they take us over completely.

We got along fine after that and I felt as if God had lifted a heavy burden from my shoulders. From that time onwards we worked and ministered together in love and we ended up actually liking each other. He went on to become an able minister of the gospel and my love and respect have grown towards him over the years.

A few weeks later the Spirit of God spoke to me as I was waking up. 'Peter, I want you to go to the Embankment,' he said. I didn't question why. I just told Barbara that I was going up to London and that I wasn't sure when I'd be back.

It was strange seeing the old familier haunts and the old familiar faces. I stayed for a few days, sleeping rough on the bench I'd slept on years before. I had a good time sharing the love of Jesus with some of my former companions. They could hardly believe that I was the same Peter Newman they had once known. The weather was still cold—it was Easter time—and I spent many a moment thinking of home, Barbara and little Elaine. But God hadn't given me permission to catch the train back to Worthing, so I stayed on the Embankment waiting for his next set of instructions.

I didn't have to wait long. Three days later I was walking along the Embankment towards Charing Cross Station when God spoke to me. He directed me to a phone box. 'Remember when you were a little boy of four?' whispered the inner voice. I remembered. I had a mental picture of Grandad taking me by the hand and walking me from Chelsea, over

Battersea Bridge, to a house one Sunday morning. I was taken up to a room and left to play on my own with some building bricks. Then Grandad reappeared and took me home.

'I want you to ring those people up,' said the voice.

'But Lord,' I said, 'that was years ago and I don't even know their name. They could even be dead by now.'

The name Mascall came to me so I opened up the telephone directory. There weren't many Mascalls listed and one of those had a Battersea address, so I dialled the number, wondering what on earth I was going to say. I half hoped no one would answer the phone, but God had other plans. The line clicked and a man's voice said hullo.

'Hullo,' I said, rather nervously, 'is that Mr Mascall?'

'Yes, this is Mr Mascall,' the voice replied.

'Well, er, this is Peter Newman here,' I said. Then there was silence. 'Er, don't you remember me?' I said.

'No, I'm afraid I don't,' said Mr Mascall. 'Who did you say you were?'

'Peter Newman. My grandad, Mr Walter Newman, used to know you.'

'Ah yes, Walter Newman. I knew him, but I'm afraid he's dead now.'

'Yes, I know that, Mr Mascall. I'm his grandson, Peter. I became a Christian a few years ago and I'm in London at the moment and I'd like to see you.'

'Oh, *that* Peter,' said Mr Mascall, sounding excited, 'Yes, yes, you must come over straight away. We'd love to see you.'

So I walked to their little terraced house along the route that Grandad had taken me all those years before. I even recognized their street as soon as I came to it. When I arrived at their home, they were waiting on the doorstep to greet me, with tears in their eyes. They could hardly believe that I was who I said I was. They took me into their little sitting room—it was just as I had remembered it—and they kept asking if I really was Peter Newman. The more I assured them that I was, the more they cried. They asked me if I remembered the day my grandad had taken me to see them and I said that I did.

They told me that while I was upstairs playing, they had spent the morning praying with Grandad.

'And do you know what?' said Mrs Mascall, 'we prayed that you would grow up to love the Lord Jesus and that God would call you to become his servant to preach the gospel. And now look at you . . .' her voice tailed off.

'Yes,' said Mr Mascall, 'your grandfather thought a lot about you, and he prayed for you, but I think he gave up towards the end because every time he heard anything about you, it was bad news. You were either in prison or were drinking and stealing. We nearly gave up hope, too. But we decided to carry on the praying and now,' he said, his voice breaking with emotion, 'I thank God we did.'

We sat and talked all afternoon. I told them how God had saved me and about Barbara and my daughter. They seemed to cry all the time and I must admit I felt very tearful too. I had some tea with them and then knew that God had done what he'd planned and that I was free to return to Worthing.

Barbara was thrilled when I told her what had happened during my visit and a few weeks later I took her to meet the Mascalls.

I made other trips to London during our stay in Worthing. One Saturday evening God told me to go to Hyde Park Corner. That morning I'd been attending some meetings in London and I was due to catch the train home. However, I knew better than to argue with God, so I found some digs and went to Hyde Park the next morning. Speakers' Corner was crammed with people and orators were spouting forth about everything from politics to religion.

I walked around until I found the spot where the gospel was being preached. There were two men there and only about six people had stopped to listen to them. They were having a rough time, too, with a couple of hecklers. As I stood and listened to them, the Spirit of the Lord came upon me and I felt a great urgency to get up and preach. I walked over to their box and asked if I could have a few words. They were reluctant to hand over their platform but I was so insistent that I almost ordered them off. When they saw that I meant business, they handed their platform over to me. Under the anointing of the Holy Spirit I started to preach about Jesus. Within minutes the six had grown to twenty, then to fifty and before long there were hundreds of people listening to the gospel being proclaimed. The crowd was silent. There was no heckling or jostling—God's word was having free course.

When I'd finished, I handed the platform back to the two preachers and walked down Oxford Street. 'Hey, come here you!' someone shouted. I turned around and saw a policeman. 'I don't know who you are or what you've got but I've never seen the crowds at Speakers' Corner listen so intently to anyone before. Where were you trained?'

'Nowhere,' I replied, 'and that wasn't me speaking. It was the Lord Jesus—he's the one who's been speaking to those people.' The officer looked at me blankly, then said good morning and went on his way. I carried on walking, thrilled that the Lord had been pleased to use me in such a way.

We stayed at the commune for several months before moving to a small evangelistic mission based in Bristol. We moved into a two-bedroom terraced house which always seemed to be full of people. We'd lived with others and now it was our turn to be the hosts. During the day I'd preach in the streets and visit the law courts to gather in the outcasts who had fallen by the wayside. I felt very fulfilled because instead of digging drains, I was doing the true work of an evangelist.

We both felt that God was using us to bring others to himself. Every morning we had a prayer meeting in the little mission hall. All sorts of people flocked to it, and as the weeks went by we started seeking God on behalf of others. What's more, we saw God answering our prayers for both converts and more helpers.

A lot of people used to come to me for counselling too, and God started to teach me about the gifts of revelation and knowledge. At the beginning of each day he would show me just who was going to turn up on the doorstep for help and what their problems were going to be. Now the problems they told me about were often different from the ones God had shown me—people like to keep the unsavoury things about themselves hidden from view—but as I shared with them what God had already revealed, they would open up and admit their real problems. God was then free to help them and put them straight.

One day a man turned up at our morning prayer meeting in a particularly bad mood. He often used to pop in to see us although he wasn't a Christian. I suspect he liked the cup of tea and biscuit we gave him afterwards. Anyway, in he walked and announced: 'I'm fed up with you.'

'Oh,' I said, 'are you? Tell me why.'

'Well, you're always saying that God answers prayers, but he doesn't answer mine.'

'What have you been asking him to do for you?' I asked curiously.

'I want a job,' he replied. Well, you could have knocked me down with a feather. I knew that a job was one thing he didn't really want. He'd been living off social security for years and was well known in the area for being a waster. I thought that if I took him to a job, carried him there and did half his work for him, he'd still complain at the end of the day. Nevertheless, the challenge was there. He wanted a job so we were going to pray one in for him.

'Let's bow our heads,' I said. 'Father, you heard all that Jock has said about wanting a job. He wants one today. Will you find one for him, please?'

Jock hung around the mission hall until lunchtime. I gave him some money to buy some lunch and told him he ought to get himself down to the labour exchange to see if there were any jobs going. He took the money, muttered something under his breath about not expecting miracles and then closed the door behind him.

'Father,' I said quietly, 'it's up to you. I can't do anything.'

That evening, as I was opening the doors for the meeting, Jock pushed his way in. It was bucketing down with rain outside and he was soaking wet and very angry.

'What's the matter with you, Jock?' I said, half expecting the worst.

'I'll tell you what's the matter with me,' he snarled back, 'I've got a job, that's what.'

I could hardly contain myself. God had answered our prayers. 'Well, praise the Lord, that's wonderful, Jock,' I said.

'Wonderful, is it?' he said ungratefully. 'Well, I may have a job but I can't go to it. I was on my way to the Labour Exchange when I stood on a pile of rubbish to look over on to this building site. The gaffer thought I was up to no good, but when I told him I was looking for work he offered me a job there and then. Said they were short handed and that I could start tomorrow morning. I told him I could—but I can't. How can I work on a building site with only a pair of plimsolls on my feet? I ask you—it's impossible, and they're all I've got!'

'That's no problem at all,' I said, 'you can have my shoes.' In those days I had two pairs to my name. One pair let water in so I wore them in the mission hall and I kept my best ones for outdoor work. I gave Jock the waterproof ones. He only kept the job for a week and I never saw the shoes again, but at least he couldn't say that God didn't answer prayer.

When I got home after the meeting that night my feet were soaking wet. Barbara asked where my best shoes were and when I told her that I'd given them away she wasn't too pleased.

'Peter,' she said with a hint of despair in her voice, 'you know we're going to a wedding this weekend and we can't afford to buy you another pair of shoes. And you certainly can't go in those old things,' she said, pointing to the soaking wet ones on my feet.

'Well, I've done it now, dear,' I replied, 'it's no use worrying about it,' and off I went into another room out of the way.

'Father,' I said as I stared into the fire, 'you heard what the missus said.' He told me not to worry because a pair were on the way. Even as he told me, there was a knock on the door. Barbara answered it and ushered in a man. He had a parcel under his arm.

'Have you got my shoes in there, then?' I asked, not daring to look at Barbara's face.

'How on earth did you know that there are shoes in the bag?' he asked incredulously. 'As a matter of fact I have brought them for you. I was having a clear-out and decided I had too many and I felt I should bring them round to this house. I hope they fit you all right.'

'Oh, they'll fit all right,' I said, 'God knows what size feet I've got.' Needless to say, they fitted.

One evening the phone rang and the duty officer at the medical mission in Bristol asked me to go down because they were having difficulty with a drunk. When I got there I found an Irishman who was loudly demanding money and making a general nuisance of himself. He said he needed cash to travel back to his home in Ireland but I felt he just wanted to go back to the pub. He gave me his sob story, obviously hoping to con me, not knowing that I wasn't going to be conned and that anyway I was broke too.

I let him ramble on at length before putting my cards on the table. I was in the middle of telling him that there was no way he was going to get any cash that night when God spoke to me and told me to go upstairs to the nurses' flat and borrow some money until the following day. I was to give the money to this man. I excused myself and went upstairs.

I was a complete stranger to the nurse who answered the door but when I told her who I was a flicker of recognition crossed her face. 'Oh, so you're Peter Newman,' she said, leading me into her sitting room. I told her about the man downstairs and asked if she could loan me some money until the following day.

There was a gleam of triumph in Paddy's eyes as I handed him the cash. I explained to him that God had told me to get the money for him and that God had promised to repay it the following day. I then told him that he was handling God's money but that

God left him free to do what he liked with it.

'So you can either go to the pub or go home on it and thank God for caring enough about you to give it to you.'

I never met that man again. The following day someone gave me some money and it was the exact amount I'd borrowed from the nurse. A few weeks later I met some Christians from Paddy's home town and they said that he had started his journey home that night and had started a new life too. He gave them a message for me—they had to tell me that he was grateful for the money and that he had found God.

God's ways definitely are higher than our ways, and once again God has shown me that obedience was the key to blessing.

Life in Bristol was hectic. For several weeks we held a crusade on a bomb site opposite one of the roughest secondary schools in the area. People told us to hold it anywhere but in that particular spot. However, we felt God had picked it especially for our work. We had a word with the headmaster and he agreed that some of his pupils could come across for some of our afternoon sessions. Honestly, those kids terrified me! They would swagger in, sit at the back and snigger at the singing. We had 'No Smoking' signs up all over the place but they insisted on lighting up.

One afternoon their ring-leader was being particularly obnoxious and I decided that it was time something was done. So, with shaking knees, I handed the meeting over to my friend Arthur, walked over to this cheeky-faced youth, plucked the cigarette from his mouth, nipped it and pushed the remainder behind his ear. All the other teenagers were watching him to see what his reaction was going to be. I think he was too shocked to do anything, and from that time onwards we developed a new relationship with our school party.

God used to move in those meetings and many people from the neighbourhood got saved. But our crusade was only scheduled to last a couple of weeks and sadly we packed up. None of the churches in the area would co-operate with us because we were the 'odd lot' who had a lot of singing and dancing in their meetings. And the established churches were suspicious of the baptism in the Holy Spirit. So when we left, the new converts had nowhere to go to, which really upset me. Jesus tells us to make disciples of all men. It's no good leading people to the cross and then leaving them there. New converts have to be fed and nourished just like little babies. All I could do was to pray that God would keep his hand on their lives and that the fruit would remain.

It was at this time that our second daughter, Sharon, was born in Tavistock, Devon. Her birth coincided with a tent crusade that I was conducting with two other brothers. We were there for ten days, and we preached in the streets, knocked on the doors, prayed and sang and shared in the tent at night. Nothing moved; the heavens were like brass. I was concerned in my heart that we had made a mistake. Should I have been near my wife at this time? Nine days and one more to go: no sign of anyone being stirred about the things of God, and no sign of the new baby. My heart was heavy—only one more day and I could be with Barbara. I felt as though we had fished all night and caught nothing. We continued to fast and pray and the last day was spent in silence and prayer, each one with his own thoughts.

The final meeting started with a few more visitors than previous nights. There was an atmosphere like there often is before a storm. As the singing didn't seem to be going too well we decided to cut it short and preach the word. I began to open my Bible and was only saying what the Bible says, when pandemonium broke out among the people. Chairs went flying in all directions while one person ran out of the tent screaming. I shouted to a pastor, 'Catch him and bring him back!' But, wonderfully, others were running to the front of the tent. The battle in the heavens had been won and people were born again.

What a night for Barbara too, as in Devon there was another struggle going on and our second daughter was finally born.

12

'I Ignored What God Was Saying'

God was calling me into the villages of England to preach the gospel, and the man who had just so kindly given Barbara and me some tea was going to help that vision come to pass. 'This is the man,' the Spirit said to me, 'who is going to provide you with the necessary money. I have told him to give you five hundred pounds.' I needed to buy a tent, a couple of caravans, a van and some chairs; and the chap who was sitting opposite me was going to foot the bill, even though he was struggling to say yes to God about it.

'The type of life you lead isn't particularly good for your wife and children,' he said to me while his wife and mine went into the kitchen to wash the pots after tea. 'You should be offering them something more secure. You've told me about your tent mission—now how on earth is someone in your position going to finance something like that?'

He wasn't getting hot under the collar with me—he was in the wrestling ring with God and I knew who was going to win in the end.

I just sat there and listened to him rant and rave for a further ten minutes. Then, all of a sudden he stopped in mid-flow and said: 'I'll give you three hundred and fifty pounds.'

Now, he knew and I knew and God knew that that just wasn't enough. So I challenged him. 'How much?' I asked indignantly.

'Oh, very well then,' he said, talking not so much to me as to God, 'I'll give you five hundred pounds.'

So once again Barbara and I saw the hand of God move on our behalf and I was thrilled that he was making the crooked places straight for us.

The week before, God had shown me the caravan I was to buy for the mission. I'd been driving past a garage when I saw it. I stopped the car, and a woman—probably the owner's wife—walked over to ask me what I wanted. 'That caravan,' I said simply. 'Oh, I'm sorry, sir,' she said, 'It's already sold.'

'Oh,' I said, 'has it been paid for?' She told me that it hadn't, but that the man who was buying it had promised to call for it the following week and that he would be paying for it then. I felt sure that he never would collect it because God had it earmarked for other uses. So I told the woman that I'd ring the following week and that if the man hadn't come up with the cash, I'd have it. So, with my five hundred pounds safely in my possession, I rang her and ended up buying two caravans.

God provided more money for us too. I remember him telling me to go and stand on a certain street corner and within minutes a man appeared, an evangelist I'd known for some years. 'Oh, it's *you*,' he said, and handed me ten pounds. He later told me that God had just spoken to him and told him he wanted to give him a hundred pounds but that he first had to give his last ten pounds to the first person he met as he rounded the corner. After handing me the cash he walked on—and someone stopped him and handed him a cheque for the needed amount.

So it was with great excitement that Barbara, myself, our children and our small evangelistic team set off. We were to hold our first mission in Cornwall—exactly where, I wasn't sure, so I asked God to lead us by his Spirit. We stopped at a hill, called Kit Hill, well known for its views of the area. I got out of the van and was having a quiet word with the Lord when suddenly I saw a ball of fire descending from the skies just above a small village. At first I thought it was a plane on fire but then I realized that God was showing me where to hold the first revival tent meetings. God even showed me a picture of the field where we were to pitch our tent. Two of the girls in the team went off on their scooters to ask the farmer if we could use his land. He said yes.

So we put the tent up and then blitzed the whole area with leaflets announcing our arrival. I couldn't wait for the first meeting and at seven in the evening, half an hour before we were due to start, I was anxiously pacing up and down outside the tent waiting for the crowds to arrive. They didn't. The adult population of this village weren't very interested in this band of non-denominational 'odd bods' who had arrived in their village to preach some sort of strange gospel. But the children in the area thought differently—they arrived in the tent in clusters of threes and fours, so we had our 'revival meeting' as planned.

On the third night a little girl came up to me before the meeting and said to me: 'Uncle Peter. My mummy says my brother is dying and would you go to the house to pray for him?' I stood silently for a minute. Now, I knew that God had healed the sick in Bible times, and I'd prayed for Barbara once or twice when she'd been ill, but I'd never publicly prayed for the sick. I'm not even sure if I believed that God would answer my prayer of faith because I didn't feel that I had much faith for healing. But here I was in a dilemma—I had to go and pray for that little boy or the mission would lose all credibility.

'Yes, I'll come and pray for your brother,' I heard myself saying to the little girl who was gazing so hopefully at me.

She took me by the hand and off we went. We arrived at her house and her mother opened the door to us. She looked terrified of me and, looking back, I can't blame her because I think I must have looked half-scared to death myself.

She took me over to the cot where her two-year-old son was lying. He was very ill and had been having six epileptic fits a day. I took a deep breath, prayed over him and made my exit as quickly as possible. That night I told the team that if that little boy died, then we would have to pack our tent up as quickly as possible and make a hasty retreat. I hardly slept a wink. I kept thinking of all the people we'd witnessed to on the streets of that little village and how they'd all be laughing at us if the boy died.

I could hardly think straight the following day. We didn't hear a thing about how the little boy was and I was too terrified to go to the house and ask. Half an hour before the meeting was due to start I asked Arthur, one of the team, if he wouldn't mind just popping over to the house to see how the boy was. Arthur, fearless as ever, left at once, only to return again within seconds. 'Peter,' he shouted, 'there's about thirty people heading this way. I think they're coming to the meeting.' Yes, I thought to myself, to lynch us all.

They all filed into the tent and sat, hands folded on laps, waiting for us to begin. I still didn't know the fate of the boy, but I had something else to worry about—how was I going to get through to all these solemn looking people?

'For goodness' sake, Arthur, play something,' I whispered dramatically. Off he went to the piano and started to belt out a couple of choruses. Now these people had never been in a meeting in their lives before. One look at them was enough to tell you that. They just sat there wondering what was going on.

I couldn't bear to watch so I ducked out of the tent for a few words with the Almighty. 'God,' I said as soon as I got outside the tent flaps. 'I don't know what to do or what to say. Please help me.'

In seconds the Spirit shared his thoughts with me. 'See that branch over there?' he said. I turned my head and saw a branch which some kids had broken off a beech tree. 'I want you to take that into the meeting and preach on "I am the Vine".'

So I grabbed the six-foot-long branch and crawled under the tent flap dragging it behind me. If the congregation had been surprised by Arthur's choruses, they were even more surprised by my entrance. Come to think of it, Arthur seemed a bit stunned too.

I plonked the branch in the ground at the front and read the story of the vine from St John's Gospel. Then I snapped off some twigs, threw them down and said: 'That's you. Dead. No life, no sap, no nothing; you're without God.' As I continued, one by one they fell to their knees crying, putting their lives right with God.

That was the beginning of the revival. It turned out that the little boy had been miraculously healed. Word spread like wildfire round the village. People came to the meetings from miles around and every night the Spirit of God was poured out on to dry and thirsty land. We just stood back and watched God have his way.

Since then God has often used me for healing, but sometimes he has kept me on tenterhooks. I remember praying for a woman in Plymouth who had a withered hand. After I'd said the prayer of faith she looked down at her hand, exclaimed that it hadn't been healed, waved it in the air for all to see and stormed out. I prayed fervently that she wouldn't come back to any of the meetings because she was bad for my faith. I also told the Lord that I was upset by the affair. I was very relieved when she didn't show up the following night, but my heart sank as she walked into the tent on the third night. I knew that she thought I was a fake, and when they saw her unhealed hand others would doubtlessly agree with her.

I kept looking at her out of the corner of my eye during the meeting and I held my breath as I made the appeal. Sure enough, she got out of her seat and I was sure that she was going to make a scene. I called a local pastor over and asked him to take her to one side if she started to cause any trouble. Imagine my surprise when she ran down to the front full of the joys of spring. She was praising the Lord and waving her hand in the air—a hand which had been made perfectly whole. She told us that she had gone to the meeting that night to expose us as frauds, but as she was singing choruses her hand had been healed.

We saw many wonderful miracles during those times—God moved mightily and set many people free. I was thrilled to be in the Lord's service and my enthusiasm knew no bounds. I used every means I could to preach the gospel. In small towns and car parks I used to hide under the back seat of my big old Wolsley car and play Pat Boone records over a loud-speaker attached to a record player. People used to throng around to see what was going on, and then I would preach. I was often told I was a public nuisance. And I'm sure I was.

We made a habit of holding open-air meetings during the afternoons, much to the annoyance of the general public. One afternoon a man threw up his window and told us to push off. He was very angry and swore at us quite a lot, but we continued preaching the gospel.

'You're disturbing my Sunday peace,' he hollered over at us. 'Sir,' I said, turning towards his open window, 'there is no peace for the wicked.'

I thought he was going to have a heart attack, such was the colour of his face. But I carried on preaching, feeling sure that someone was going to get saved that afternoon.

Out of the corner of my eye I spied another man watching from his window. The Spirit told me to preach to the irate man, but said that the other man would get saved. Sure enough, down came the second man, crying to God, and God, as always, answered his cry and the man found peace.

Seeing God move more than made up for the discomfort and inconvenience of the travelling life. Barbara didn't complain once during those months, although her life was far from easy. She not only looked after her family and the team, but she also had to listen to my complaints when things weren't going right.

Sometimes hecklers came to give us a hard time, but I welcomed them because I saw them as a challenge. We were the target of abuse and stones many times, but none of it seemed to matter. God was using us, we were doing the work of an evangelist, souls were being saved and bodies healed, so what more could we ask for? I felt that we were successful in God and I liked the feeling very much indeed.

So you can imagine my surprise when God told me to end the tent mission. 'I'm doing a good job here, Lord,' I told him, 'and I must go on preaching.'

So go on preaching I did. I ignored what God was saying to me and I told the team we were moving to another village in the South to hold some meetings. We arrived and started putting up the tent. The others were out giving leaflets to the villagers and I was tackling the awesome task on my own. An old man was sitting on a nearby bench watching me. He stayed there all morning, puffing away on his pipe and eyeing me up and down as I chased from one end of the tent to the other. He went away for his lunch and came back to watch my antics during the afternoon.

I eventually finished round about tea time and the old man tottered over to me and said: 'If I was you I would take that tent of yours down. If you don't do it, the wind that'll blow round this place tonight will do it for you.' It was a calm day, not a cloud in the sky. I was sure this was the enemy talking.

'That tent will never blow down,' I assured the old gentleman, 'because God has called me to preach his Gospel so he's looking after both me and my tent. I can also assure you that I'll be here to preach tomorrow night, tent or no tent.'

The old man went on his way and I went on mine. I got back to the caravan, had my evening meal and went to bed early, ready for a full day's evangelism the following day. At about four in the morning I was woken by the rocking movement of the caravan. I could hear the wind howling and in an instant I was wide awake. The tent! I bolted out of bed, pulled on my clothes and jumped into my car, giving Barbara a garbled explanation of my actions.

Our caravan was about three miles from the tent. Dawn was breaking over the deserted country roads and in the silence of the early morning I could only hear one thing—the words of the old man. I reached the village and there, on the village green, were the remains of my beloved tent. The wind had done its work. The poles were broken, the canvas was ripped, the chairs were strewn all over the place.

I started clearing up the mess in the half-light of the new day. Tears were rolling down my cheeks. The wind had started to drop and it was raining. I felt thoroughly miserable and kept tripping over the ropes and tattered canvas.

The only relief that day came from a sympathetic policeman's wife who brought me one of her delightful cornish pasties and a lot of sympathy. I needed both. God had let me down and humiliated me in this village. The old man, with his pipe, was back, silent but with a twinkle in his eye and 'I told you so' written all over his face. Several times that day I asked God why he had let this happen.

Other Christians came by with advice.

'Perhaps God hasn't called you.'

'There might be sin in your camp.'

'It was a test.'

But I knew the real reason—God had said, 'Move on, Peter, new fields lie ahead.'

That night, standing in the pouring rain with a piece of the remaining canvas wrapped around me, I preached the good news. My text was 'He will have his way in the whirlwinds and the storm.'

It's hard to give up something which God is blessing. For two years we'd seen miracles and I'd been slow to hear God pronounce his benediction on the work. The truth of the matter is that it had become *my* tent and *my* ministry and I had wanted to keep it. But I finally had to bow the knee to God. All right, I told him, my tent days are over. But what next? I went to Kit Hill to pray and fast and to find out what was to be our next step.

13

Shut Up in a Room

'Brother Newman,' the man said as we all prayed in a large room in Holland, 'God is going to make you into his donkey so that he can ride on your back.' Stupid man, I thought angrily. I hadn't fasted and prayed for nine days to hear something as dull and uninspiring as that.

I'd gone to Holland with some Christians I'd met, shortly after waiting on the Lord on Kit Hill. I felt that God would answer me on that trip to Holland, so I shut myself away to seek him. I prayed, fasted, read my Bible and spoke in tongues, but the only result seemed to be nausea and headaches—until that morning meeting when a brother came over to prophesy over me. I was quite prepared to dash back to England and book the Albert Hall, but when he started to talk about donkeys my heart sank. A race-horse, yes, Lord, but not a tatty old donkey ambling from one assignment to the next. I can't describe exactly what happened in my spirit at that point, but I do know that something within me seemed to die. I was prepared to be many things for God—I'd been called a fool for Christ many times—but I wasn't prepared to be his donkey.

I left Holland a disappointed man. Somehow that stirring enthusiasm which had driven me for so long had withered up and died. My ministry began to change from that point onwards. In many ways God started to do more exciting things than ever in my life, but the bubbling joy and excitement which used to be with me was no longer there.

Instead of holding missions and meetings, God started to tell me to go places, and he always led me to individuals, not crowds. God did some remarkable things. One day I was sitting on a train heading towards Stuttgart in southern Germany. I was watching the beautiful scenery round the Rhine when God told me to speak to a young man sitting opposite. There were four of us in the compartment—myself, the young man and a married couple. I reckoned all three of them were German so I told the Lord I was going to have difficulty obeying his request. The young man, who was probably in his late twenties, stood up and went out into the corridor. I followed him.

We were standing next to each other looking out the window. 'It's beautiful scenery,' I started to say in English. He just looked at me blankly and indicated that he couldn't understand what I was saying.

'What now, Lord?' I asked.

Then the Lord told me to do a very strange thing. I had to speak in tongues! I wasn't all that keen to do as the Lord had asked, but I obediently opened my mouth and spoke in tongues. Immediately the young man started to reply in Dutch. God also gave me the ability to interpret. The young man told me he was a lorry driver travelling to Italy to pick up his lorry. He said his parents were Salvation Army officers who ran a hostel for alcoholics and down-and-outs in Amsterdam.

I then told him how God had sent me to tell him about his love. We talked for a long time. I don't know if he ever gave his life to the Lord but I, at least, had the assurance that I was in the right place at the right time.

I travelled to Africa, to Israel—all over the world. I often set off without any idea of the purpose of my journey, but I always saw God working. Yet there was still a dryness in my spirit. I felt I was doing things almost mechanically: it was no longer wonderful to serve God. Deep down I resented the fact that God wasn't going to make me another A. A. Allen, Oral Roberts or some other great world famous evangelist. There was no denying that I was becoming the donkey God wanted me to be, but my heart was still fighting him. I felt he was holding me back in some way, denying me the public profile I had become used to.

I suppose it was out of this restlessness and lack of fulfilment that our African venture was born. Barbara and I didn't feel at home in any fellowship or church in England; so when we met these loving, caring Christians who lived in a commune in South Africa, we packed our bags and with our two daughters, Elaine and Sharon, we set out to join them. It was several weeks before we realized that some things were not quite right. We had had no idea, at first, that we had joined a cult.

How could an evangelist be so lacking in discernment? Well, every Christian needs to be in close fellowship with a praying church. Wise church leaders might have seen the dangers and helped me to look more carefully before I leaped. My problem at this time was that good men of God wanted me to represent their denomination, while I was concerned more for the furtherance of God's kingdom and less for the expansion of any particular denomination.

(Today I am surrounded by men and women who have my ministry at heart, and are in a position to advise and exhort me, for which I am thankful to God.)

The commune in Cape Town seemed to offer everything we needed. They cared about us, made a fuss of us, loved us, talked about being born again. A lot of cults are harmless at first sight: it's only once you're in them that you find out their true teaching and beliefs.

One of the cult's main errors was that the members believed that their prophets were infallible and that you had to do exactly as they said. They eventually ruled our lives, even telling us which soaps to use. I took it for so long, but then I started to question and indeed disobey the 'prophets'. I was told that I was blaspheming the Holy Ghost in doing so and must repent. I refused, so I was shut up in a room for three days in a bid to make me come to my senses. Barbara, meanwhile, was in our quarters, torn between thinking they were right and I was wrong, and that I was right and they were wrong. The enemy is so very subtle, and although we'd only sat under the cult's teachings for a few months, they had already started to indoctrinate us.

Deep down I knew they were wrong, and during those three days I resolved to get myself and my family away from their influence as fast as I could. Some of my old evangelist team had gone out with us and I prayed that they, too, would break away and head home for England.

Meanwhile I pretended to repent for not listening to the prophets and I was allowed back to my quarters. Barbara and I made preparations to leave. The prophets told us that if we left we were walking out of our salvation and that our marriage would break up. They also said that our children would die.

We arrived back in England terrified and in deep depression. Satan really attacked us and I used to spend days in total mental confusion, wondering if the cult had been right and if I had been wrong. I felt I was heading for a complete mental breakdown and our marriage started to show signs of stress. I had a spirit of fear upon me. The Bible says that fear brings torment and, believe you me, it does. My spirit still communicated with God, but my mind argued that because we'd left the cult, we were destined for hell and damnation.

Shocked and depressed, feeling like Elijah underneath the juniper tree (1 Kings 19:3–4), we felt that we wanted to die. But God had called us to live, and we soon began to discover that he was faithful and continued to supply our needs. Just when there seemed no one to provide we would find provisions anonymously supplied. And there were those loving Christian brothers and sisters who saw our hurt and bewilderment and helped us and provided for us many times, giving us the love we so desperately needed at that time.

My spiritual life was maintained in the only way I knew—by continuing to witness to the love and mercy of God. I would make my way to hippie communes, and into houses that they had squatted in, and invite them to our flat for food and talks and prayer. My candle may have been flickering at this time, but I was determined that it would not go under a bushel.

This stress lasted for about eighteen months, although it took me about four years to feel free from those we had known in South Africa, but I knew that I was free when I was able to pray for them earnestly and in love. Thus my deliverance came by continuing to preach the gospel, for that is where the real power of God is made manifest. It was difficult at times, and only those who have had the misfortune to be involved in these things will know how strong those powers are that seemed continually to cling to my thoughts. But in the mercy of God what seemed terrible at the time has now become profitable in our ministry to those who have been involved in such bondages.

But meanwhile there was worse to come. We found that Christians in England didn't want to know us. Church leaders who had once clamoured to have me take meetings in their church now shunned me as if I were something unclean.

On the odd occasion that I was invited to preach,

my old 'friends' would warn people away. During those years people even said I was a spiritist and that I should be avoided at all cost! There was no spirit of forgiveness at all—the Christian gossip vine was alive with the news that Peter Newman had gone into error. The people who had once put garlands round my neck were now throwing stones.

I thank God that he is always faithful. His hand was on me right through those nightmare months and years. It was a long time before the scars were healed. Deep down I was still afraid that the things the so-called prophets had forecast would come to pass.

Meanwhile God was still using me, telling me to fly here and fly there, miraculously providing me with the cash to do so. My timetable was secret—only the Father and I knew my destinations. I remember going all the way to Ethiopia once just to cut some grass for an old missionary lady. I'd arrived in the country and had spent four or five days preaching in one village, when the Lord seemed to tell me to walk into the middle of nowhere—in Africa! I walked for what felt like ages before I came upon a group of huts. A Finnish missionary, a white-haired eighty year old lady, came out of one of them.

'This is the second time I've had to come out to Africa, brother,' she told me, 'because no one else will come out to look after these people.' She took me into her hut and gave me a cup of tea and a bed for the night.

The next morning she handed me a scythe and said: 'Brother Newman, I'm so glad God has sent you to me. I've been asking him to send me a man for several weeks now. Will you please cut all this grass for me, because it's full of snakes and the natives won't do it.'

So I set to work chopping a quarter of an acre of elephant grass in the blistering heat of the day. I later preached the gospel to the natives, but I'm sure my main reason for being in Ethiopia was to cut that old Finnish lady's grass!

I later saw many miracles in Ethiopia—especially when the Coptic Church announced over the radio that no one should go to my meetings. That, of course, made people more curious than ever and some soldiers from the nearby barracks actually broke out to hear the gospel. Many of them gave their lives to the Lord.

Yet deep down I was still dissatisfied. Towards the late sixties, after three years, God started to speak to me about my family. He told me to go to Cornwall and settle down with them—I felt sure he was going to open the door into a new type of ministry.

My two daughters were ready to leave their primary-school education, I knew that God had ordained family life and structure, and he was interested in our children and the need for them to have a stable education and to make permanent friendships. Up to this time we had been continually on the move, living in other people's homes and in communes. This was not the first time that God had shown us that we should protect our children from feeling hard done by because we were committed to the call of God. They had to share us with so many people; they knew what it was to have drunks sleeping in their home, not to mention drug addicts and many others with psychological problems. It was nothing for one of them to be seen sitting on a tramp's knee, or to go with him for a walk in the park. Often they would have drug addicts teaching them art. They learnt from an early age that our life was a life of sharing and our house, cupboard and pocket were always open to those in need. Though often poor in this world's goods, they became rich in God's love and grace. My great joy today is to know that my children know Jesus and love him.

14

An Evangelist, Not a Social Worker

A farm set in the heart of beautiful Cornwall became our new home. The building itself was fairly dilapidated but neither Barbara nor I cared—it was home, cracked walls and all. I'd been right about the new ministry too—we were hosts to drug addicts and alcoholics.

We were scared stiff of the first drug addict who arrived on our doorstep. We'd been expecting him, so we had carefully decorated his room to make him feel welcome—our bedroom was in a terrible state but his was like a palace. Within days of arriving he had painted obscene pictures all over the walls and put filthy captions underneath them. My eyes almost came out on stalks when I first saw them, but I decided that as he was obviously trying to shock me, the best thing to do was to ignore his works of art completely.

We repeatedly told him that our home was his home and that he should treat it as such. He must have taken us at our word because he tried to burn the place down by setting light to a stove in his bedroom. We managed to put it out before too much damage was caused.

We eventually had up to sixteen men and women sharing our home with us. Some of them were saved and allowed the Lord to straighten their lives out for them, while others just went their own sweet way. We needed a lot of grace, wisdom and understanding in dealing with them. Our first rule was not to push the gospel down their throats. I never once stood up and preached to them as a group, but I was quick to take every opportunity to chat about Jesus with individuals as we worked side by side in the fields or the barns.

In early 1967 I was very busy again taking meetings at home and overseas. As always my type of ministry brought me into contact with those on the other side of the track, and I was keen to help them in a more practical way, to make some provision for them other than meetings. I continually came in contact with other people involved with the welfare of drug addicts and began to sit around a few drug centres that had been set up by the medical profession. One of these was in Chelsea, London, the borough that I was born in, and this centre was in a Salvation Army Hall.

The Officers involved in the work encouraged me to go ahead, and when we finally got started some of the Officers came down to the farm and were a great help and encouragement in the beginning.

The one person that was a real help to me throughout all my ministry, especially in the setting up of the farm, was David Foot Nash. Right from the beginning of my tent days he would provide me with equipment as well as spiritual advice. As his profession was that of a solicitor he was able to advise me on many things, and it was by his expert advice that we were able to purchase the farm. There were quite a few problems concerning this, but by prayer and David's skilful handling it was purchased and a company was formed. I had a £1 share in the company plus, as David said at the time, all the responsibility to keep it going.

Once we got started and people got to know of our place we were continually being contacted by other drug centres, the probation services, psychiatrists, and even judges phoning direct from courts before they decided what to do with a person. Christian ministers of all denominations would phone us—often late at night, as well as the Samaritans and the police. When we were approached by likely candidates we tried to make sure that they had been through most of the rehabilitation programmes and had not responded. The reason for this was that, although we were not professionals in this field, we offered these dear people a *home*. Not a hostel or a rehabilitation centre, but something they could know as *their* home and not just ours. Many of them had difficulty with this at first, but when they got the message they began to take an interest in the place and to share some of the responsibility. Their attitudes towards society often changed and they were able to listen and relate to others.

Because most of our guests were addicts, they were very cunning and determined to cling to their habits. Several of them used to try to grow their own cannabis in odd corners of the farm; the Lord used to show me, by his Spirit, where these hiding places were. Once I'd found them I would wait until the growth was well under way, then I'd attack it with weed killer—never letting on to the lads what was happening. Baffled by the sudden death of the plant they would start all over again, and so it went on.

The nearest pub was six miles away, but distance was no object. One day I was standing by an upstairs window when George came staggering up the path on his way back from the boozer. He'd had a skinful and was carrying a bag in his hand which I knew was filled with bottles. I watched him look around, then hide the bag in a hedge before sauntering into the house. I nipped down to the kitchen to wait for him. He came in, straightened himself up and said: 'Hi, Peter.'

I said, 'Hello.'

He stretched, yawned, then said he was going upstairs for a lie down because he was feeling a bit tired. He wasn't going to admit that he'd been in the pub and I didn't let on that I knew.

I waited until he was asleep before going to the hedge and rescuing his two bottles of cider. I hid them in my room and then went back to the kitchen.

George reappeared after an hour or so. 'Hi, Peter,' he said, still trying to look as if he hadn't been drinking. 'Where are all the others?'

I told him they were all out blackberrying so he said he would go and join them. He picked up a saucer, of all things, and headed outside. I saw him make for his hedge. He searched and searched and eventually headed back to the farm, with two blackberries in his saucer.

'Where did you say the others were, Peter?' he asked. I told him they were in the fields at the back of the farm. He didn't bother trying to join them but later that night, when we'd finished our evening meal, he slid up to me and whispered confidentially: 'Peter, we've got a thief in the house.'

'Oh,' I said, 'why George, what have you had stolen?'

'Oh, nothing, Peter, but there's definitely a thief in the house,' he replied.

'Well, you aren't telling me anything I don't already know,' I told him. 'After all, George, all of us have stolen at some time or other and we're all capable of doing it. So what have you had stolen?'

He wouldn't say, but I'll never forget the look on his face when I called the gang into the kitchen the following morning. Whenever I found drink on the premises I used to publicly pour it all down the sink. George's two bottles of cider ended up in the Cornish drainage system too—but at least he knew who the thief was!

The lads also tried to make a still in one of the barns. I had great fun watching them trying to keep it a secret. They used to go into unholy huddles and there was a great feeling of conspiracy in the place. At night I'd go into the barn to inspect their handiwork. I could see that their contraption would never yield a drop of whisky.

I took a multitude of jobs to keep the farm going. Christians round about viewed us with suspicion and

I admit that I still harboured bitterness against my fellow believers. The scars of South Africa and our home-coming were still there.

While we didn't have a hundred per cent success rate with our guests, we enjoyed a reasonable degree of success. During these six years I became quite an authority on rehabilitation and was asked to speak about our work on radio and television. We were visited by social workers and probation officers, and I was often in court speaking on behalf of the guests. Some courts even sent boys to us, and I enjoyed being popular for once in my life. During those years my spiritual life was quietly dying—prayer was becoming a thing of the past and that close fellowship which I had once enjoyed with the Lord was crowded out by a busy diary.

I believe that God had led us into that particular work but Peter Newman, as usual, had tried to take it over. I had once had a vision of Jesus, yet there I was, hardly able to pray, cut off from God. Unsaved people thought I was marvellous. I was invited to sherry parties and official receptions. I stood by and listened to dirty jokes without batting an eyelid. I even heard the name of God blasphemed and didn't once open my mouth in his defence. Outwardly I was a success, yet inwardly I was experiencing a spiritual desert.

Sometimes I would think back to the days when I moved in God and felt so close to him. Nothing, not even seeing drug addicts going straight, could match that feeling. Every now and again I would feel the presence of God, but then it would go, leaving me cold and empty.

In my spiritual bewilderment, I went into business with another man. I invested nearly £4,000 in plant to hire out. For the first couple of years it went well. Then people couldn't pay their bills on time, and as we had to pay large amounts of hire purchase to the firms which had made the machines we ended up in a big financial mess.

But in the midst of all this turmoil God started to get hold of me again. I knew that I was like Jonah running away from God's call. I also knew that, like Jonah, I was very bad company for those around me, so I told my partner that I was pulling out. I told him that it was for his sake, but he didn't understand. I signed all the machinery over to him and I accepted responsibility for all the debts, because I felt it was my fault that we had them in the first place. Money, at that time, didn't matter to me. God was again speaking and moving in my life.

Quite simply, he was telling me that he had called me to be an evangelist, not a social worker.

15

The Donkey Is Going to Be Loosed

Barbara, myself and our children moved out of the farmhouse into a small cottage up the road. I then spent the next fourteen months waiting on God and listening to what he had to tell me. He completely reshaped my thinking and believing and I eventually came back to a simple faith in Jesus. There I was—a failure, broke, almost homeless, an ex-member of a cult, and yet there was God—blessing me! For years I'd struggled and striven but over those months God showed me how to enter into his rest. You don't have to be always up and doing for God in order to justify your salvation. You can sit back and relax in his presence, but when he tells you to move, then move you must. I came to realize that the world *is* in the palm of his hand—and if the world is there, then I am too. My soul had been thirsty for years and I simply enjoyed drinking from God and relaxing at his feet.

There were external pressures—my business failure was constantly rearing its head and court proceedings were threatened. But in a way I didn't care. I had once again found the pearl of greatest price, and nothing, but nothing, was going to distract me from my relationship with God.

In order to eat, I used to go into the woods and cut logs which we would sell from our front door. I would take my dog, Prince, with me and we'd spend many an hour talking to God in the forests. Barbara was relieved that I, at least, was starting to see straight again.

God also dealt with the bitterness which I was harbouring in my heart against my fellow Christians, and I spent many hours ringing people up, apologizing to them for my resentments.

I remember the first meeting I was asked to speak at during that great cleaning-up period. I preached the simple gospel message and the power of God came down to touch many hearts and lives. I made the appeal and my daughter Elaine was the first to get out of her seat. 'Dad, I want to be saved,' she said. With tears in my eyes I led her to the Lord.

I'd spent about eighteen months just waiting on God, learning of him. Then he started to open doors. From different parts of the country by post and telephone people began to invite me to take meetings, and people began to arrive at the house for prayer and help. It was just like the old times and I was surprised and a little overawed by it all. But deep inside I knew it was God that was doing this. Something new was stirring and the feeling in my spirit was confirmed six months later at an International Gospel Outreach convention at High Wycombe. A friend of mine persuaded me to go with him, but I was reluctant. I'd spent a long time in the desert without too many Christians around and I quite liked my isolation. An added incentive to stay away was the fact that everybody there would have doubtless heard about my South African venture and I was loath to have it all dragged up again. But God had decided that the convention was to be holy ground for me.

The first night I was there God told me to join International Gospel Outreach. I'm not one to join things for the sake of it, but God spoke very clearly to me about it. The IGO is really a fellowship of ministers from established non-denominational churches and it exists to encourage men in the work of God. So I applied to join and they put me, like everyone else, on twelve months' probation to prove myself, and to make sure that I wasn't preaching any sort of heresy.

David Greenow, one of the founders, asked me to say something at the convention. I obliged, albeit reluctantly, and a brother called Eddy Smith, whom I didn't know, came forward to pray for me. He began to prophesy and said that the key I'd been searching for was at hand. Now I'd told Barbara several weeks beforehand that I was searching for the key to enter into God's rest, and here was this stranger telling me my innermost thoughts.

'Brother Peter,' he said, 'God wants you to be his donkey. He's going to ride your back like he rode on the back of the ass going into Jerusalem. People aren't going to see you, but they're going to see Jesus. . . .' I could hardly believe my ears. God, ever faithful, ever patient, was again telling me what he first told me some fifteen years earlier. Only this time

I bowed the knee and I had no ambitions to be a gleaming racehorse ever again. I was to be a donkey. His donkey.

We left the convention the next day and went to a house fellowship in Wales. My immediate reaction was, 'God, what am I doing here? It's too much like a commune for my liking.' But God knew what he was doing.

My friend preached on the Saturday night and the next morning I woke up and said to him, 'Arthur, today the donkey is going to be loosed.'

'Well, I'm sorry I shan't be here to see it, Peter. I'm off today.' So Arthur went and I stayed behind.

That evening in the meeting a brother looked across at me and said: 'Peter, I don't know what it means, but God is saying that the donkey is going to be loosed today. You're the donkey and God's going to ride on your back.' Talk about out of the mouth of two or three witnesses!

He'd barely got the words out when in walked a woman with a bowl of water and a towel. I thought that someone had been sick at the back of the meeting. But she came up to me, took off my shoes and socks and washed my feet, just as Jesus washed the disciples' feet. As you might expect, I felt very embarrassed. Then God spoke to me and said it would happen twice again to me before he would lead me into the final ministry that he had for me.

From 1976 onwards God really began to move in my life. He opened doors, did the impossible, performed miracles and led me to many different countries. Yet all the while I sensed that it was preparation for the work he was going to have for me.

I became God's donkey, going here and there when he told me to go. I learned that there's no need to fret or fuss in God's will. I've nearly been in three plane crashes, but I can honestly say that I've not panicked. I've just committed my way to the Lord.

Since my earliest days I've known that if things didn't seem to be working out I had to stand still and wait on God. I also learnt to use every day to the full. There is no clocking on and off; God's Spirit neither slumbers nor sleeps, and often keeps unsocial hours.

Years ago I looked around my Gospel Tent at oil lamps and broken chairs. 'God,' I said, 'if only I had an electric generator, then I could have brighter lights.'

'Use what you have to the full, Peter,' was his reply.

I also discovered that God expected me to do a bit of practical work from time to time to earn money. I would look around for a house that needed painting and offer to paint it. During the day I would paint the house and at night preach. It certainly made an impression on the local community and they got to hear the choruses as my unmistakable voice boomed from the top of the ladder: 'At the cross, at the cross, where I first saw the light.'

It has been fun to see the hand of God in my travels and there are quite a few enjoying the blessing of God because I just happened to take my blow lamp and wrenches along. I have collected dead animals, dug and built cess-pits, driven cars across South Africa and fished on a trawler in the Irish Sea under the guidance of God, becoming all things to all men that I might win some for Christ.

After preaching at a large denominational church I was standing at the back shaking hands as the people left, but one dear gentle lady withdrew her hand as I took it to shake. She looked at me and declared that she had never met a preacher with such rough hands.

I never chose this path and I have had some rows with God over it. What has hurt most has been when this ministry of working for a living has been exploited by other Christians and they have used me for cheap labour. But it has been a thrill to go in with my tools and skills and do jobs for people who couldn't afford to employ anyone.

I was once down in a manhole, arm up a four-inch pipe, having left a note on the toilet seat saying 'Please do not use', when to my dismay I heard someone pulling the chain. In my hurry to move my arm, it got stuck.

I was at this time being observed by a well-known preacher. 'I don't know how you do it,' he exclaimed.

I replied, 'Cess pit or pulpit, as long as God's presence is with me, it is heaven.' And I meant it.

I've often found that God uses me most while I'm travelling from one place to another. I remember landing at Los Angeles and thinking that I would contact some Christians I knew in that city, when God told me that I had to spend the night in the airport itself. I did—and ended up preaching the gospel there. The glory of God fell, and at one stage I was dancing before the Lord with a nun by my side.

Towards dawn God told me to go across the lounge and pray for a man who was sick. So I went up to him and started chatting to him about the Lord Jesus Christ. He, in turn, poured out his troubles to me and told me of his illness.

'I can see you're sick, sir,' I said to him, 'but God has sent me over to you to lay hands on you because he's going to heal you.'

'Yes, but I don't believe in that sort of thing,' he said to me.

'Oh,' I said, 'I'm sorry. Perhaps I've made a mistake, sorry to have troubled you. . . .' And with that I walked away from him.

I asked God if I had made a mistake and he told me that I hadn't and that I had to go and pray for the man. So off I went again.

'Sir, you'll have to excuse me, but you're in a bad state both physically and spiritually. In fact, naturally speaking, you've just about had it. But Jesus has told me to come back and to lay hands on you. He wants to heal you.'

The man looked quite startled. 'Oh well,' he said, 'go ahead, I suppose.' So I laid my hands on him and prayed. Within seconds he bounded up, saying he was healed.

'What you felt was the Holy Spirit. Now God wants you to give your heart to him. Give yourself to him completely and he'll give you a new heart,' I said, and the man willingly complied.

How great is our God!

16

The Place of Rest

Many of my lessons have been learnt through pain, trial and tribulation; some self inflicted. Barbara and I have experienced many hardships in the call of God—hunger, bankruptcy and having all our possessions stolen are but a few. Many times we have almost fainted by the way. We are given to understand from the word of God that the trial of our faith is precious to him. I can't say that I have found it precious to me at the time. Nevertheless the end result of these trials has always revealed in greater depths the faithfulness of God.

It may often seem to the onlooker that my life is free of trials and tribulation now that I have found the place of rest which for sixteen years I laboured to enter. I found it by returning to the simplicity of the gospel and resting on God's word. This has taken away the stress of living; it is the stress and strain that wears most people down. Much of the tension was caused when I tried to live up to a standard that others demanded of me and struggled to convince everyone that I had arrived at the place of rest. This became filthy rags in the eyes of God but, praise his name, God had the answer even to my filthy rags.

However, God has continued to give me the opportunity of praising him under difficult circumstances: I'm not immune from trials and pressures. I'm sharing this with you, not so that you can commiserate with me, but that you may be encouraged to press on towards the prize of the high calling in Jesus.

We have in our family two daughters and one son, Jonathan, who is the youngest. We have seen the healing power of God working in the lives of our daughters and raising them up from sickness. When our son was born it was discovered that he had a problem with his kidneys. He was operated on when he was four years old and for a couple of years he was well. But then he began to deteriorate rapidly, till by the age of eight he was in chronic renal failure.

Hundreds prayed for him, and still are praying. During the course of my ministry I have prayed for many children of Jonathan's age and God has healed them, yet we have had to watch him suffer through the years. There were times when we panicked, when we felt the heavens like brass. All my experience over the years, the memory of all the wonders God has performed, have screamed at me, 'What about your son? Where is God in this?' But then the Holy Spirit has risen up from within my innermost being and has begun to glorify and praise the name of Jesus.

Much advice has been given. Some people have suggested that I should not pray for the sick until God has healed Jonathan, and I have often felt like following their advice. Some have told me that I must be in sin or pride or out of the will of God. I believe that suggestions like that do not come from the heavenly courts, neither can they be found under the New Covenant that God made through Jesus Christ to all those that believe. Jesus Christ came to destroy the works of the devil. I believe that sickness and anything that would seek to destroy a man's faith in the word of God comes from Satan himself or from very ill-informed people.

We have, however, learnt many lessons through Jonathan's illness and I would like to share one with you.

In prayer one day God spoke these words to me: 'Peter you don't really love me.'

'I do, Lord!' I replied.

'No, Peter you only love me because.'

'What do you mean "because"?' I asked.

'You love me because—I found you; because—I saved you; because—I healed you; because—I called you.'

At this point I was beaten.

'Lord, show me your love!' I cried.

Several months later I was in Great Ormond Street Hospital sitting by my son's bed. He had tubes up his nose and into his arms after yet another operation. Weeks of tests, reports and counter-reports had driven us almost to despair. We had prayed and so had almost a thousand others during those weeks. Yet in the end we had had to watch them wheel him into the operating theatre to cut him open for 'further investigation'.

I had sent Barbara away to try and get some sleep,

and so was by myself as Jonathan recovered from the anaesthetic. His first words when he came round were, 'Dad pray,' and he began to whimper because of the discomfort he was in.

'Son,' I said, 'your dad's all prayed out, I don't even know what to pray for.'

He looked at me and said, 'Dad, give me a drink of water.'

I was under instructions to give him the tiniest drop of water every hour.

He had already had his quota for that hour and had forty-five more minutes to wait before the next drop was allowed. I panicked and decided I couldn't stay with him. I couldn't bear to see him suffer. My mind said, 'Run, leave him to the nurses.' But the Holy Spirit said, 'Pray.'

There by that hospital bed I called on the name of the Lord. I said, 'God, help me, I don't know how to handle this situation. This is my only son and I love him but I can do nothing for him.'

Then God spoke. He said, 'Peter, now you know and feel my love. I too had a son hanging on a cross. When he cried to me I hid my face. Because I loved the world I gave my son.'

I can only say that at that moment everything changed. The holy love of God, and his peace came into that room. What had seemed an unclimbable mountain suddenly became a molehill. More than that, God told me to give Jonathan a wet cloth to suck, and he went to sleep.

Two years later my son Jonathan left hospital once again, after another operation. When we were in the car he said, 'Dad, God is good to me!'

Now as he sat there all I could see with my natural eye was a young boy chained to a life line which would restrict him from living a life that many other young boys enjoy. So my reply to him was, 'Son, how is God good to you?'

'Well, Dad, it's like this: one, I'm going to have a meal at the Little Chef. Two, there are lots of children left in hospital, and they don't have mums and dads that know the Lord and many of them are sicker than I am. That's why God is good to me, Dad.'

There are many unanswered questions, and there always will be this side of heaven, but we are not aiming to spend eternity down here; we look for a city whose builder and maker is God.

17

God in the Fire

Jonathan's illness had come to dominate our lives, and even though hundreds of people were praying, there seemed to be no intervention from God. Three years after Jonathan's operation, I decided to give Jonathan one of my kidneys. I felt it was the most natural thing in the world for any father to do for his son.

No, I didn't know what I was talking about. I didn't understand what such an operation really involved. The doctor was most hesitant. He looked at me and saw age—grey hair and wrinkled brows. However, though he knew about my faith, he didn't know my God. Sometimes God invites us to meet him in the fire, as he met Meshach, Shadrach and Abednego in the time of Daniel.

So God overruled human decisions and the initial tests began.

How dehumanizing—getting undressed, needles, samples. But I soon adapted to the system. I got over the embarrassment of carrying my sample from one department to another; even needles came to mean nothing to me, though the first time a nurse took a drop of blood from me I just about fainted.

There was one obstacle in the way of the transplant, and that was the insistence of the transplant team that I see a psychiatrist. This is the normal procedure for all potential donors. Now I had very strong views about this profession, none of them complimentary, and so I refused to go along with the system. An appointment was made which I never kept and, hearing nothing, I thought I had got away with it. But I seemed to be waiting a long time to get the date for the transplant, so I made enquiries and was told in no uncertain terms that unless I saw the psychiatrist there would be no transplant.

So I made the appointment.

Of all the tests that I had prior to the transplant this was the one that I approached with the most apprehension and suspicion. 'Watch it, guard your tongue,' I thought. 'Perhaps he'll think you're a religious nut.' 'Just answer yes and no,' was my last piece of advice to myself, as I entered Dr Enoch's office and sat down on a chair.

'What, no couch?' I thought. But after Dr Enoch had introduced himself I felt we were old friends and there was the presence of Jesus, known only to those who have been born again. The psychiatrist turned out to be my brother in Jesus!

As he began to tell me of his faith and how he believed that God had placed him in his profession, I thought, 'Peter, you've blown it again and limited God to your own understanding.'

The day came when they gave us the date of the transplant. Jonathan and I got really excited. All results were positive. Nothing would be sure until the last day, but boy, we were pleased. I saw worried looks on people's faces when I told them the good news, but I couldn't wait. I had found God in this fire, so fear and worry had no hold on me.

Before the transplant I had to enter the hospital for a minor operation. Nothing to it, I discovered; they gave me an injection to calm me down, a 'pre-med', and I felt as high as a kite!

'Dad,' said Jonathan one day while we were impatiently waiting and he lay in bed having one of his bad days.

'Yes, son?' I replied.

'Dad, when the surgeon takes your kidney and puts it into me, it will give me a new life.'

'Yes, son, it will give you a new life because it will purify your blood.'

'Dad, that's what happens when Jesus comes into our lives. He gives us a new spirit and makes us clean.'

'That's right, son.'

'Praise God,' I thought, 'what a sermon!'

'Dad, now I know what it *really* means to be saved.'

At last the day arrived. Transplant: eight o'clock in the morning; we were to be the first in the operating theatre. Six o'clock: bath, painted nearly all over with iodine.

Soon, I thought, they will give me that pre-med shot and I will get high and go down to the theatre singing.

The porters came to wheel me down. 'What about the pre-med, nurse?' I asked. 'Have you forgotten?'

She looked at the notes.

'Nothing here, Mr Newman,' she said.

God, what are you doing? I'm supposed to have a pre-med. Everybody has a pre-med. Don't you know, God, I'm supposed to be sedated? I, of course, meant 'high', but I didn't like to tell God that.

I lay in the waiting room outside the theatre and it was cold. The central heating had failed. Everybody full of apologies. More blankets, please.

As the lady doctor took my details, she turned to the nurse and said, 'Has he had his pre-med?'

'No,' said the nurse. 'It's not on his notes.'

Immediately the doctor took off to see the surgeon. How relieved I was that action was being taken. The doctor returned, looked at me and said, 'I'm sorry, there's been a slight mistake. You can have the pre-med, but it won't have time to work because the surgeons are ready for you now.'

'Let's go,' I heard myself say.

Wide awake, I was wheeled in. I think I counted five figures all masked up. As soon as they had lifted me to the table they began to stick things on me and in me. I really began to believe that not only were they going to deny me my longed-for drug, they were also going to deprive me of my right to be put to sleep while they operated! Wrong again, I'm glad to say.

'What's this pain? God, where am I? What's happening?' I tried to move but was stopped by pain. Somebody was putting another needle in my stomach! Can one find God in pain? For the first time in my life I was about to find out. In my walk with God I had come to know many kinds of pain—the pain of guilt, loneliness and rejection—but physical pain I had not yet encountered. When praying for the sick I had often felt that to identify with their suffering it would help if I knew physical pain. Well, if that was to be a qualification for praying for the sick, I had now qualified.

I slowly came round from the anaesthetic and became aware of my surroundings; pipes, people and . . . pain. My first anxious question was, 'How is Jonathan?' Joy and anxiety were bound together. I had had a kidney removed. It had actually happened —that was joy. But had the transplant worked? Was my kidney active in Jonathan?

When I arrived home, leaving Barbara and Jonathan behind in the hospital, I was really ill. I was nearly a stone lighter, and I had only weighed ten stone when I went in. The pain and the weakness had taken their toll, together with other problems that I had to face which were far worse, and more painful. One serious problem was that I thought that death was stalking me, and twice I felt my spirit leaving my body. I would have willingly gone, except that there was something wrong. I believe that when my eternal spirit has to leave this tabernacle, then angels will escort me to the presence of God, but my experience at that time was different. All I could see in my mind's eye were demons fighting to drag me away, taunting me to curse God and die. They reasoned with me that not only had my friends forsaken me in my darkest hour, but so had God. I always tell people that when the father of lies tells you that God has left you, then it means that God is near at hand. If God has truly gone, the devil will leave you alone.

There came a morning when all strength had gone

and I just could not summon up the will to hang on any longer. Then suddenly there was light and power in that bedroom, and there was my own sister, Daphne, speaking in tongues and confessing the blood of Jesus. There is nothing that will cause the demon power to back off more than the presence of one of God's children, full of faith and the Holy Spirit.

Daphne had arrived at our home in 1959, desperate and defeated, sustained by tranquillizers, deceived by spirits, having been enticed into spiritism, sanctioned by men but forbidden by God. Then the Great Shepherd saw her need and stretched out his hand to set her free.

From that time on I began to mend and soon got back to fighting weight. At the time of writing this it is six months since the transplant, and Jonathan continues to get better. Barbara has found it strange, not having to spend so much time nursing him, and we have really appreciated our new freedom.

Barbara has had to bear the brunt of this affliction in our family, and to have the two of us in the operating theatre at the same time was a great trial to her faith. Once again God has proved faithful in giving me a wife who has stood firm even in the darkest times.

18

'I Am Just About to Shoot You'

I have continued travelling and going wherever the Holy Spirit leads me. I have always found it a trying experience, to be led by the Spirit. As soon as I am bidden to go I immediately find a dozen reasons why I can't. I think, 'Where's the money coming from? Will any one turn up when I get there? It's your own imagination.' I hear voices shouting the odds against my going. Then finally Satan will start at me. That gets me going quicker than anything. That's when unbelief and fear fly out of the window. If the father of lies, the great deceiver, tells me not to go, then that's the time to go.

When I arrive at places—unexpected and uninvited—it does my soul good to hear the words, 'Brother, the Lord has sent you.'

One of the things I have begun to notice is that my ministry is changing and I am being directed more into the ministry of prophetic utterance.

This really made me nervous at first. Had I not been warned to beware of false prophets? And I, too, had warned people. Yet here was I proclaiming to many people things that for the life of me I did not understand myself. I will share just one event so that you may understand my feelings about this new ministry.

I was in a large meeting and after having preached and prayed for a number of people I was approached by a young woman who was quite agitated. In her distress she poured out her story. Her husband was in prison and was taking out papers to seek a divorce on the grounds that they couldn't have any children, because she had taken drugs.

As I was praying for her I heard myself saying, 'This time next year you will have a baby boy.'

Someone shouted out, 'Praise the Lord', but all I could think about was how to get out of the church as quickly as possible.

Eighteen months later I was back in that church. I had forgotten about the previous incident. If I had remembered I don't think that I would have accepted the invitation without making a few discreet enquiries first.

After the meeting was over, I was approached by the same young lady. I must confess that I panicked when I heard her saying, 'You said that I would have a baby boy in twelve months.'

'Lord, I've had it now,' was my immediate thought.

But she continued, 'I couldn't bring him tonight, he's too young. My husband came out of prison and got saved. Six months ago we had a baby boy and we've called him Joshua.'

I heard a loud voice say, 'Praise the Lord.' It was mine.

In a meeting in England the words came loud and

clear, 'Brother Newman, I have shaped you and sharpened you into a fine arrow and I am just about to shoot you on target.' I thought, 'So that's what God's been doing with me all these years: shaping and sharpening me! No wonder it's been so painful at times.'

I've already told you about my first foot-washing experience. I had completely forgotten that God had told me this would happen on two further occasions.

I was in America when, after a meeting, a woman crept up to me and whispered that God had told her to bless my feet. I was astounded to say the least, and I felt the same awe mingled with embarrassment.

Later the women told her story. Eighteen months earlier God had spoken to her and told her that he required her to bless an evangelist's feet. Being shy and nervous, she thought that she would never have the courage to carry it through. So she confided in a few friends. She said that at every meeting she went to, she dreaded that this would be the time when she had to obey God. Finally she came to one of my meetings and God showed her that I was the evangelist—and she could not do it. When she arrived home she felt that she had disobeyed God, and could not put things right, as she heard that I had left the area.

But, as always, God is good and bigger than our mistakes. Through unforeseen circumstances I stayed over, and she arrived at another meeting to find I was unexpectedly speaking. This time she was obedient, but only just. She said, 'It's not easy to obey the Spirit of God, for often he asks us to do the most unusual and childlike things.'

Yes, there was excitement in my spirit. God had told me that the foot washing would happen three times, so there was one more to go. It had been four years since the last time. How long before it would happen again—four years or forty?

Only four weeks later I was having lunch in a house in Jacksonville, Florida when, as we were preparing to leave, in came a sister with the now familiar bowl and towel. There was no embarrassment on my part this time, I endured it joyfully.

What will happen next? Where will God lead me? What will he do? I do not know the details. But I do know that, since the very earliest days when Grandad prayed with Mr Mascall, God has honoured prayers and fulfilled his will for my life. Sometimes, because of my rebellion, this has taken a long time. But God's faithfulness never wavers, not even for a moment.

It's for him to lead: my job is simply to follow.

Also in paperback from Kingsway . . .

In Search of God

---

by David Watson

The world is depressing: meaninglessness, apathy, frustration and loneliness prevail. Man is the centre of his own greatest problems—not the government, husband or wife, or career, but himself. He gropes amid failures and broken relationships in the search for happiness. Is there a remedy, or just the sure approach of death to contemplate?

David Watson, who has been greatly used by God in parish ministry and missions at home and abroad, has a deep conviction of the need for Christ in society today. His preaching has influenced thousands, and this book will be read and reread by all those who have not closed their minds to the existence and love of God. Its powerful undercurrent touches nerve-endings and demands a response.

My God is Real

by David Watson

If the things Christ said are not true, then the sooner we throw this Christianity into a funeral pyre the better....

On the other hand, if Christ's teaching is the truth, the position is very different. There may need to be radical changes in our lives, a new life altogether. What is necessary is that we should know what real Christianity is all about: and that is the purpose of this book.

The Cross Behind Bars

The true story of Noel Proctor—
Prison Chaplain

by Jenny Cooke

As a boy, Noel Proctor thought that God didn't live outside the Sunday School classroom. Until something happened that was to turn his life upside down and launch him into a totally unexpected career: chaplain to one of Her Majesty's prisons.

Noel soon discovered that he couldn't convert the hardened inmates of Britain's prisons singlehanded. God had to do a deeper work in his life before revival could come to the nation's 'forgotten people'.

This is the warm and intimate account of how one man learned to live in the power and will of God, and how his wife found the courage to fight 'terminal' cancer. Above all it shows how God's power can be released when his people put him first in their lives.

Noel Proctor *held chaplaincies at Wandsworth, Eastchurch and Dartmoor Prisons before becoming Senior Chaplain at Strangeways in Manchester.*

Jenny Cooke *is an adult education tutor who teaches creative writing. She is married with three children.*

Kingsway Publications

How to Live the Christian Life

by Selwyn Hughes
author of *Every Day with Jesus*

Do you
wish the day was over before it has hardly begun?
get irritated by even the smallest problems?
find reading the Bible every day difficult and tiresome?
have trouble mastering temptation?
try to copy others instead of developing your own gifts?

We can cram our heads with doctrine, but that in itself will not keep us from the problems that rob our lives of the peace, joy and effectiveness that Jesus promised. This book points the way through such problems, helping us to become the kind of people God intended. It is a positive affirmation that we *can* get the best out of the Christian life.

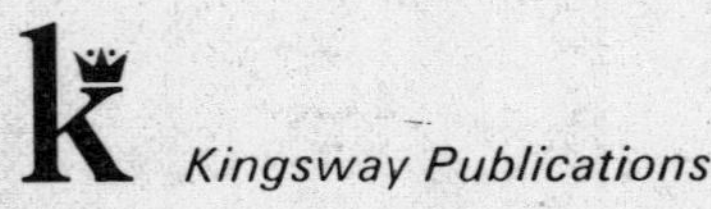